A Practical Guide to Teaching English in the Secondary School

A Practical Guide to Teaching English in the Secondary School offers straightforward advice, inspiration and support for all training and newly qualified secondary English teachers. Based on the best research and practice available, it offers a wide range of tried and tested strategies and practical activities to ensure success in the secondary classroom.

Illustrated throughout with examples of good practice and activities to promote careful thought, the *Practical Guide* covers key aspects of English teaching, including:

- effective lesson planning and pupil progress;
- getting started with drama;
- teaching poetry successfully and enjoyably;
- media education and media studies – an introduction to the curriculum and designing schemes of work;
- teaching English Language;
- choosing and using fiction for all ages;
- teaching English Literature at A Level;
- opportunities for ICT in English;
- planning meaningful assessment.

A Practical Guide to Teaching English in the Secondary School is an essential companion to the best selling *Learning to Teach English in the Secondary School*. Written by expert professionals, it provides detailed examples of theory in practice, enabling you to analyse and reflect on your own teaching in order to ensure pupil learning is maximised. Providing a combination of practical ideas, educational rationales and activities to stimulate personal thought and development, this book explores a wide range of issues pertinent to the teaching and learning of English in the twenty-first century.

Andrew Green is Senior Lecturer in English Education at Brunel University, where he leads the PGCert in Secondary English Education. He is author of numerous literary articles, books, and teaching resources as well as academic papers on the subject of English A Level and Higher Education English. He is a Fellow of the Higher Education Academy.

Routledge Teaching Guides
Series Editors: Susan Capel and Marilyn Leask

Other titles in the series:

These Practical Guides have been designed as companions to **Learning to Teach [subject] in the Secondary School**. For information on the Routledge Teaching Guides series please visit our website at www.routledge.com/education.

A Practical Guide to Teaching English in the Secondary School

Edited by
Andrew Green

Routledge
Taylor & Francis Group

LONDON AND NEW YORK

First published 2013
by Routledge
2 Park Square, Milton Park, Abingdon, Oxon OX14 4RN

Simultaneously published in the USA and Canada
by Routledge
711 Third Avenue, New York, NY 10017

Routledge is an imprint of the Taylor & Francis Group, an informa business

British Library Cataloguing in Publication Data
A catalogue record for this book is available from the British Library

Library of Congress Cataloging in Publication Data
A practical guide to teaching English in the secondary school / edited by
Andrew Green.
    p. cm. — (Routledge teaching guides)
    Includes index.
    ISBN 978-0-415-67505-5 (pbk.) — ISBN 978-0-203-10105-6 (ebk.)   1. English
language—Study and teaching (Secondary)—Great Britain.   2. English
literature—Study and teaching (Secondary)—Great Britain.   3. Education,
Secondary—Aims and objectives—Great Britain.   4. Curriculum planning—
Great Britain.   I. Green, Andrew.
    LB1631.P67 2012
    428.0071′2—dc23

                                                                    2012007175

ISBN: 978-0-415-67505-5 (pbk)
ISBN: 978-0-203-10105-6 (ebk)

Typeset in Palatino and Frutiger
by RefineCatch Limited, Bungay, Suffolk

Printed and bound in Great Britain by the MPG Books Group

Contents

CONTENTS

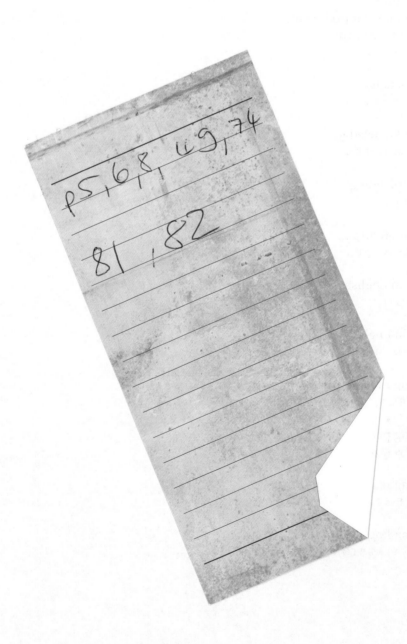

List of figures

Contributors

Carol Atherton teaches English at Bourne Grammar School in Lincolnshire, where she is also Director of Professional Development. She has written widely on the teaching of English Literature post-16, the transition from school to university and the history of English as an academic discipline.

Andrew Green is Senior Lecturer in English Education at Brunel University, where he leads the PGCert in Secondary English Education. He is author of numerous literary articles, books and teaching resources as well as academic papers on the subject of English A Level and Higher Education English. He is a Fellow of the Higher Education Academy.

Carmel Kellett spent 17 years teaching English and Literature in a variety of 11–18 schools before becoming a PGCE tutor at the University of Manchester. She also has many years' experience as a senior examiner for both GCSE English and Literature. Her most recent role is as a subject advisor for a group of schools on behalf of a leading exam board.

Ishmael Lewis is a lecturer in the South West Wales Centre for Teacher Education where he works on the PGCE English programme and the MA(Ed). His particular interests are language development, talk based learning and Philosophy for Children. Prior to this, he taught English for many years in schools in South Wales.

Elizabeth Ridout has been the leader of the English Faculty at Carshalton High School for Girls, a large comprehensive school in a London borough, for more years than she cares to remember. During that time she's seen government ministers and changes in the curriculum come and go but still believes that English, taught well, can change lives.

James Shea was Head of English at a Humanities Specialist Secondary School for ten years before taking up his role in 2008 as Senior Lecturer in Secondary English for the Department of Secondary and Post-Compulsory Education at the University of Bedfordshire with a research area of New Technologies in Education.

Rob Smith is an Advanced Skills Teacher of English at Westwood College, a 13–19 school in Leek, Staffordshire, and an Associate Tutor specialising in the teaching of English and Drama at Manchester University. He is editor of *The Merchant of Venice, King Lear* and *Julius Caesar* in the Cambridge School Shakespeare series.

Linda Varley taught and examined A Level English and Language before joining the University of Manchester in 2002 as a PGCE Tutor and course director for an M.Ed. course on The Teaching of English. She is currently Joint Programme Manager for the *Teach First* North West PGCE programme, which she combines with her role as Professional and English Subject Tutor. Her research interest is the 1944 Normandy Campaign and she has designed and resourced a website for Normandy veterans recording their first-hand experiences.

Series editors' introduction

This practical work book is part of a series of textbooks for student teachers called the *Routledge Teaching Guides*. It complements and extends the popular generic book entitled *Learning to Teach in the Secondary School: A Companion to School Experience*, as well as the subject-specific book *Learning to Teach English in the Secondary School*. We anticipate that you will want to use this book in conjunction with these other books.

Teaching is rapidly becoming a more research and evidence informed profession. Research and professional evidence about good practice underpins the *Learning to Teach in the Secondary School* series and these practical work books. Both the generic and subject specific books in the *Learning to Teach in the Secondary School* series provide theoretical, research and professional evidence-based advice and guidance to support you as you focus on developing aspects of your teaching or your pupils' learning as you progress through your initial teacher education course and beyond. Although the generic and subject-specific books include some case studies and tasks to help you consider the issues, the practical application of material is not their major focus. That is the role of this book.

This book aims to reinforce your understanding of aspects of your teaching, support you in aspects of your development as a teacher and your teaching and enable you to analyse your success as a teacher in maximising pupils' learning by focusing on practical applications. The practical activities in this book can be used in a number of ways. Some activities are designed to be undertaken by you individually, others as a joint task in pairs and yet others as group work working with, for example, other student teachers or a school or university-based tutor. Your tutor may use the activities with a group of student teachers. The book has been designed so that you can write directly into it.

In England, you have a range of colleagues to support you in your classroom. They also provide an additional resource on which you can draw. In any case, you will, of course, need to draw on additional resources to support your development. Other resources are available on a range of websites, including that for *Learning to Teach in the Secondary School: A Companion to School Experience: 5th Edition* (http://cw.routledge.com/textbooks/9780415478724/), which lists key websites for Scotland, Wales, Northern Ireland and England.

We do hope that this practical work book is useful in supporting your development as a teacher. We welcome feedback which can be incorporated into future editions.

Susan Capel
Marilyn Leask
Series Editors

Acknowledgements

I would like to thank my colleague Fay Weldon for permission to use extracts from the script of her television adaptation of *Pride and Prejudice* which appear in Chapter 6, and Jenny Grahame of the English and Media Centre for agreement to adapt and use ideas initially published with the editor in *Becoming a Reflective English Teacher* (McGraw-Hill, 2011). I would also like to thank Rhiannon Findlay of Routledge who has provided timely and invaluable assistance in preparing this manuscript in the final stages of publication.

Abbreviations

EAL   – English as Additional Language
GCSE – General Certificate of Secondary Education
HE   – Higher Education
HEI   – Higher Education Institution
HOD – Head of Department
ITE   – Initial Teacher Education
IWB – Interactive Whiteboard
KS2 – Key Stage 2
KS3 – Key Stage 3
KS4 – Key Stage 4
NC   – National Curriculum
NQT – Newly Qualified Teacher
PGCE – Postgraduate Certificate in Education
QTS – Qualified Teacher Status
S&L   – Speaking and Listening
VLE – Virtual Learning Environment

With the exception of Chapter 10, where Advanced Level learners are referred to as 'students', the word 'pupils' has been used throughout this book to denote children in schools.

Chapter 1 Introduction

ANDREW GREEN

As a teacher of English, you face many exciting challenges and some big responsibilities. English, as set out in the National Curriculum (NC), is a wide and varied subject. It covers a broad range of content material as you will see in Chapter 2, as well as a variety of functional skills. English functions as a subject in its own right, but also (more than any other subject) operates as an underpinning structure for pupils' learning across the whole of their schooling. Access to any and every subject is through the word, written or spoken, and success across the board, therefore, depends upon the abilities pupils learn through their study of English.

For this reason, it is important to enter your reading of this book with some key questions in your mind:

- How do I see English as a subject? Literature? Language? Media? Text-based? Theory-based? A combination of the above?
- How do I achieve a sensible balance between the skills English teaches and the wide variety of content it also encompasses?
- How do I develop my own range of understanding in the subject?
- How can I approach the teaching of English to make it a stimulating and fulfilling experience for my pupils?

Activity 1.1

Questions

Look at the questions above and jot down your initial responses. As you read on in this book, return to these questions and your initial responses regularly. How do your answers to these questions develop as you read, and why?

Add any further questions of your own that you wish to consider as you work through the book.

It is hoped that this book, which sets out to emphasise the practical dimension of the English classroom, will enable you to develop provisional responses to these questions and any others you may have, and in so doing make you a stronger thinker about your pedagogic practice. Learning about teaching is an iterative process, however, and knowledge about teaching will continue to develop throughout your career. Personal philosophies of subject, pedagogic practices, understanding of and response to curriculum or exam specifications will, quite rightly, develop as you develop as a teacher. This book, therefore, does not seek to give a set of hard and fast answers about how to teach English – such hard and fast answers simply do not exist. What it does seek to do is to provide a challenging introduction to a range of topics as a stimulant to personal thought and a set of approaches you may wish to explore in your own teaching context.

To begin your thinking, here is a set of four issues relating to professional practice as an English teacher that are taken as principles for this book:

- *Competence* – you owe it to your pupils and to your employer to demonstrate competence on all occasions in the teaching of your subject. This means not only knowing the subject content of your lesson well (i.e. do you know the topic or text you are teaching effectively), but also providing suitable learning activities that relate clearly to your objectives for learning, understanding how your work relates to the National Curriculum and/or relevant examination specification, monitoring and assessing pupils' work regularly and accurately, developing pupils' work in each of the four modalities, etc.

- *Creativity* – it is important both for your pupils and for you that your classroom is an exciting and stimulating place to be. This means thinking hard about the range of creative activity that pupils undertake within their learning: knowledge is not to be 'delivered' in the impoverished parlance of current educational discourse, as if it were some neat little package, it is to be created and explored, and you as a teacher need to think about how you can make the conditions for this in your classroom.

- *Classroom disciplines* – it is important that your classroom provides a good learning environment for pupils across the full spectrum of ability. This will mean developing a variety of strategies for dealing with undesirable behaviour, but it far more often means thinking about the kinds of good study disciplines and procedures (when working as an individual, as a group and as a whole class) that will make your classroom a safe and constructive place to be. You as the teacher are the person who must set the tone for this and must develop working practices that will ensure all have the opportunity to succeed.

- *Clarity* – it is important that you are always clear about your purposes and requirements. Sometimes this will be invisible to the pupils – like the swan gracefully gliding across the surface of the lake, not everything that goes into your lesson planning will be or should be evident to pupils – but pupils must always know clearly what you expect of them, both in terms of the work you expect them to do and the behaviour you expect of them.

As you read on, think carefully about how these issues emerge and what they mean for you as you develop your own practice. It is not the purpose of this book to provide you with a set of right and wrong answers – such a thing is not possible; teaching is an intensely personal activity, the success of which depends upon you as an individual learning to work the best you can with the range of classes you teach. What works well with one class may not work well with another. In fact, what works well with one class on Monday morning, might not work well with the same class on Thursday afternoon. However, by applying the above ideas rigorously to your thinking about teaching English, you will become increasingly expert in your judgements and will maximise the pleasure that you and your pupils can gain from the shared experience of 'doing English' together.

Chapter 2   Subject knowledge

ANDREW GREEN

In this chapter you will consider:

- your relationship with English;
- your personal philosophy of English;
- your knowledge of the content of the National Curriculum for English;
- what subject knowledge entails;
- cross-curricular English;
- what you need to do to develop your subject knowledge.

INTRODUCTION

English occupies a unique position within the English education system. It is simultane-ously a subject for study (it has a wide range of content as set out in the NC for KS3 and KS4 and in examination specifications post-16) and medium of study (the language, written and spoken, through which pupils must engage with learning and be assessed on their learning). This double focus creates certain tensions for teachers of English, as there is a constant pres-sure for them to raise pupils' skill levels – as exemplified in the push for Functional Skills – sometimes at the expense of more imaginative and stimulating content. It is very impor-tant, therefore, that you as a beginning teacher think carefully about how these two elements of the curriculum can operate symbiotically within your teaching rather than becoming competing forces. It is clear that pupils must be taught the basic skills they need to function linguistically as learners, but learning in English comprises much more than this.

PERSONAL PHILOSOPHY OF SUBJECT

Before going on to explore the content and philosophy of the National Curriculum for English (NCE), it is important to establish what you yourself understand by English as a subject and think what you want to achieve through teaching it. Whether you have worked in schools recently or not, you have already had a wide range and many years of pedagogic experience as a learner of English – at primary school, at secondary school and most recently at university. All of these experiences will have operated in you to establish your own views of English – what you like and dislike, how you view the relative importance of literature and language as issues for study, how comfortable you feel about teaching grammar, your opinions regarding teaching media, or how you feel about the use of drama in the English classroom.

These personal prior experiences of learning (and perhaps teaching) English will all have a significant impact on your views of the subject and how you wish to approach the teaching of it. As such they form a major element of your subject knowledge, not only in terms of content, but also in terms of pedagogy and attitudes. In order to understand how you can most effectively work with your pupils it is first important that you understand your own relationship with English.

Activity 2.1

Your relationship with English

Devise a table similar to the one at Figure 2.1 to explore your own memories of English. Respond as honestly and in as much detail as you can to the statements. Feel free to add further statements if you wish. Try to remember how you felt at various stages in your career as a student of English, and take time to think about how these experiences might influence your own teaching.

Statement	Personal experience	Likely impact on my teaching
I was allowed the freedom to develop my own views about language and literature.		
I was encouraged to play with text and explore its potential both in reading and writing.		
Speaking and listening were valued as highly as reading and writing.		
My English teachers/lecturers enthused and inspired me.		
I was encouraged and enabled to read widely for study and for pleasure, and love reading in a wide variety of genres.		
I enjoyed the process of writing and developed into a confident and regular writer in a wide variety of forms.		
I learnt how to be a confident, autonomous student.		
My teachers/lecturers used a wide variety of pedagogic approaches (including drama and other active approaches).		

Figure 2.1 Your relationship with English

Having thought through your own experiences of English at school and university and the formative influence these experiences have had on you as a beginning teacher, it is now important to convert these into a personal philosophy for teaching. Take time out to write down you own personal philosophy of English teaching. It is a good idea to make this a formal document to which you return at regular intervals, so that you can modify it in the light of your developing experience, or to remind you of the reasons why you wish to teach the subject. This document will, in effect, seek to capture the unique experience of English that pupils will gain by being in your classroom. Of course parity of experience is important, and the NC is an 'entitlement' document to ensure the range of coverage and the broad content of pupils' experience of English during their compulsory education to the end of KS4, but teachers' personal beliefs have an important role in bringing to life the experience of school English.

You also need to think about where your own personal views may need to change. It is not, for example, satisfactory to have a view of English that excludes poetry. Nor is it desirable to adopt a pedagogy that does not include drama as a method. Think carefully about areas of your own philosophy that might need to be challenged. Identify your own personal difficulties with the subject as specifically as possible and set aside time to think about how these issues might be reconciled. If you are on a course of Initial Teacher Education (ITE) it might be possible to discuss these issues with other members of your group and/or your Higher Education Institution (HEI) tutor. If you are already working in school, other colleagues or your Head of Department (HOD) might be good people to ask.

THE NATIONAL CURRICULUM

It is obviously important, given that most schools in the UK follow the NC (with regional variants in place in Wales, Scotland and Ireland to reflect local issues and agendas), to spend some time early in your career familiarising yourself with the details of the NC. First of all it is interesting to note how the curriculum is broken down. It is separated into sections for KS3 and for KS4, recognising that these are distinct phases of a pupil's education. KS3 represents the first three years of a pupil's secondary education, and KS4 is generally studied in years 10 and 11. For most – though not all – pupils KS4 will be when they study for their General Certificate in Secondary Education (GCSE). The division into these two sections implies that the two Key Stages are differentiated according to content and outcomes.

Activity 2.2

NC content and outcomes

Spend some time looking through the NC. This is available at: http://www.education.gov.uk/schools/teachingandlearning/curriculum/secondary/b00199101/english

Consider how effectively and to what extent the two sections of the NC relate to one another and how far they genuinely represent progression through the secondary years.

It would also be a worthwhile activity to look closely at the NC for Key Stage 2 (KS2), the upper years of primary education, in order to think about some of the issues pupils face as they make the transition from primary to secondary school education in English.

Having considered the division of the NC into Key Stages, it is then interesting to note that the curriculum is also divided into three further sections: Speaking and Listening (S&L), Reading, and Writing. This is a natural division of the subject according to the four modalities of language, and it is important to look closely at the range of coverage in each of these areas and what they are understood to encompass. However, it is also worth noting the substantial crossover that exists between these sections of the NC. Can we, for instance, make a complete distinction between the activities of reading and writing? When we engage in acts of prediction, for example, are we actually reading, or are we on some level actually writing? When we work on drafting and redrafting a piece of writing, do we not engage in complex acts of reading? Furthermore, why does the curriculum include discrete sections on Reading and Writing, but combine S&L within one? These and other questions are important to consider as you approach the curriculum. Remember that the NC is not a politically neutral document – it is an educational political manifesto – and so as a teacher of English you need to think very carefully about the political views of subject English and education it embodies.

Activity 2.3

A political curriculum

As you work through the NC, think about the political imperatives that lie behind the requirements it sets out. Here are a few key questions to consider:

- How does the NC seek to define grammar – what emphasis does it place on grammar and why?
- Look at the lists of authors in the Literary Heritage section – who is in and who is out of the compulsory lists? Why do you think this may be the case? Are any sections of the community under-represented? What might this mean?
- Is there a fair balance between literary and non-literary text?
- Are media and film fairly represented?
- Is the balance between Reading and Writing, Speaking and Listening equitable, or do some of these appear to be more important than others?

You may well have many more questions of this type. Think carefully about how the curriculum is deliberately intended to 'shape' pupils' learning in English. How does this make you feel? Is it a version of English you are happy to teach?

It is important to remember that the NC is a legal document, and its content should be covered with all pupils, unless there is good educational reason for not doing so. Within most school English departments, Programmes of Study and Schemes of Work will exist. A range of outline Programmes of Study and Schemes of Work are also available online as a starting point for your own thinking and planning. It is well worthwhile looking into a range of these in order to understand how meaningful courses can be devised to meet the progressing needs of pupils as they move through their secondary education in English. Planning needs to take account not only of immediate needs at particular points in a pupil's education, but also needs to address needs over sustained periods of time.

At the same time as the NC provides the legal framework within which English must be taught, it is important that it is not seen as a straitjacket. Many teachers talk of the NC as if it were a constrictive document they are not free to work with, but like any text it is open to interpretation. The NC should be seen as a baseline document, not as a limiting prescription. The NC, in other words, identifies the minimum that pupils are entitled to within their English education. Should teachers wish to cover additional things, they are perfectly entitled so to do. So if, for example, you wish to teach literary texts by authors not named in the prescribed or recommended lists you may. Frequently this can be done alongside the teaching of other named authors or as part of other topics. In fact, given the generous breadth of coverage within the NC, it is hard to imagine very much that could not be justified for inclusion within the Speaking and Listening, Reading or Writing sections of the curriculum. This actually allows for you, as a teacher, to express considerable individualism within your teaching and to cater to a very wide range of pupil interests. Figure 2.2 provides an indicative list of texts you may wish to cover and you should consider where they might come within the curriculum. You could also develop a similar table for other topics or issues you will cover through your teaching (e.g. book production, writing processes, textual reception, language development, etc.). For each one, try to find a location in Speaking and Listening, Reading, and Writing.

Topic	Location
Philip Larkin	
Lady Gaga	
Cereal packets	
Maths text books	
Nigel Slater	
Beowulf animated film	
Casualty	
The Simpsons	
A movie script	
An instruction manual	
Chaucer	
Illustrations by Gustave Doré (e.g. of *The Rime of the Ancient Mariner* or *Macbeth*)	

Figure 2.2 In the National Curriculum

To help you think about how your knowledge of English relates to the coverage required by the NC, it is good to undertake an audit. This should be done early in your career or course of training and should be regularly reviewed in order to ensure that you keep your knowledge current.

Activity 2.4

Auditing your subject knowledge

Look in detail at the Breadth of Study sections of the NC at both KS3 and KS4 and think about the following:

- What do you know about the topics or authors identified in each case?
- Where do you have gaps in your knowledge that need to be filled?
- What do you need to do to fill these gaps?

Discuss the outcomes of your subject knowledge audit with colleagues or with your HEI tutor, then develop for yourself an Action Plan to help you develop your knowledge.

CROSS-CURRICULAR VIEWS: RECONCEIVING SUBJECT KNOWLEDGE

English, although it exists as a subject in its own right within the NC, is a truly inter-disciplinary subject. There is a certain danger in viewing subjects as discrete entities – a danger enhanced by the paradigm construction of the secondary curriculum and by formal qualifications, which encourage pupils to separate rather than to connect their learning in different, but related subject areas.

As a teacher of English, great advantages accrue from developing cross-curricular lessons and collaborations. Such collaborations encourage teachers and pupils to look beyond the artificial boundaries between subjects established by curriculum and examinations. Such connections encourage creative porosity and enable pupils to conceive of and utilise their developing knowledge of the world in a wider variety of contexts, and more creatively. In 'London', Blake envisages humanity shackled by what he calls 'mind-forg'd manacles'. He laments the narrowness of vision that so often characterises human existence and interactions. By viewing subjects too narrowly, teachers (and as a result their pupils) can lose sight of the wider picture and the exciting possibilities of learning, because the compartmentalisation of knowledge leads to blinkered vision, lack of transferability and ultimately to the weakening of social flexibility.

Activity 2.5

Compartments

Think carefully about how your own education in English has been compartmentalised. This is often the result of modularisation of learning, which encourages pupils and students to see learning in 'units' or 'modules' or 'packages' – these are often the actual terms used – and which also allows for the avoidance of certain topics, genres or fields of learning. Students at A Level select between English Language, English Language and Literature or English Literature. Think about how different an experience of English the student of each of these options will have. At degree level, students may largely avoid the study of poetry, or may study very little (if any) literature prior to Shakespeare.

Think back over your own experience of learning English. How has your knowledge been compartmentalised?

How could you explore new connections and expand your sense of the potentials of English?

As the content of the NC proliferates, it is increasingly important for teachers of English to consider their relationship to their subject. To see English as primarily about literature (as many English teachers do) is no longer a viable position. Like it or not, the notion of text (and with it the range of what we must engage with as teachers of English) is expanding exponentially. This imposes upon teachers the need to engage more deeply with the centrality of language within English learning, and ways in which they can provide pupils with opportunities to explore this. The proliferation of content within the NC identified above highlights the need for teachers to reconceive their relationship with the subject.

Activity 2.6

Creating connections

Here are some headline ideas for creating connections between English and other subjects. Use each as a basis for creative thought:

- Consider the role of aesthetics in the Arts and in Mathematics.
- How are morality and ethics conceived in the Arts and in the Sciences?
- How do artistic movements such as Imagism, Romanticism or Dadaism emerge?
- How do such movements differ between the Arts?
- What is the influence of such movements on other social formations (e.g. political systems or scientific research cultures, or perceptions of the body?

Activity 2.6 *continued*

What new and exciting dimensions for learning does each of these ideas, or any others of your own, suggest? How could these relate to the current curricular formation of English as a subject?

These ideas and others engage us closely with Freire's ideas of critical literacy. Here we approach questions central in the study of English of how we read the world. These are powerful ideas to bring into the English classroom and into our conception of English as a subject. As teachers, we need to look for ways that we can explore with our pupils a plurality of ways of looking at and 'reading' the world. If we do this effectively, we can provide pupils with powerful knowledge paradigms rather than with 'weak' set answers and set ways of looking; we can encourage and enable them to be effective questioners of the world around them who have a variety of means of developing responses.

CONCLUSIONS

As this chapter has demonstrated, subject knowledge encompasses much more than what a teacher overtly 'knows' about his or her subject. Content knowledge is, of course, very important – pupils, their parents or carers and your employer will rightly expect you to know in detail any topic or text you are teaching – but given time and effort, the acquisition of new content knowledge is comparatively straightforward. Content knowledge, however, is only part of the picture. A range of other theoretical concepts relating to paradigms of subject, methods of teaching and learning, pedagogy and the ways in which English as a subject functions need also to be considered overtly both in and out of the classroom. (See Unit 1.1 of *Learning to Teach in the Secondary School* where I have explored these ideas in depth.)

In the rapidly changing world of language and text, where new technologies and new means of communication are constantly evolving and where the relationship between creators and consumers of text are increasingly blurred, issues of subject knowledge are becoming increasingly challenging. This places new and exciting possibilities before teachers of English, but also requires them to reconsider both the nature of the subject and the nature of how it can be taught.

RECOMMENDED READING

Green, A. and McIntyre, J. (2011) What is English?, in A. Green (ed.) (2011) *Becoming a Reflective English Teacher*. Maidenhead: Open University Press, pp. 6–25.

Green, A. and Leask, M. (2009) What do Teachers do?, in S. Capel, M. Leask and T. Turner (eds) *Learning to Teach in the Secondary School*. Fifth edition. London: Routledge, pp. 9–21.

Green, A. (2006) University to school: challenging assumptions in subject knowledge development, *Changing English*, 13(1): 111–23.

Chapter 3   Lesson planning

LIZ RIDOUT

In this chapter you will consider:

- the reasons for planning lessons;
- lesson aims, learning objectives and learning outcomes;
- the three-part lesson and its components;
- planning for the unexpected;
- potential pitfalls in planning;
- planning for behaviour.

INTRODUCTION

Sitting in the staffroom, you will hear teachers ask what their colleague has just taught so that they can do the same, or you will hear them wonder out loud what they are going to do with Year 9 that afternoon, and it may cross your mind to wonder whether these teachers who have been around for ages actually plan anything. During your ITE programme you will have been shown how to write detailed lesson plans on complicated forms and you know for a fact that no established teacher does any such thing – a glance at their planner just says 'To His Coy Mistress' or 'Act 2 cont.' in the lesson slot. So why bother? It is hugely time-consuming filling out a plan with the timings next to every task. It is exhausting having to think of new and interesting approaches to every topic, and how to provide a suitable variety of activities within and between lessons. It takes hours to compose the worksheets or the Interactive Whiteboard (IWB) flipcharts that the pupils just take for granted and do not treat with the awe and respect you think they deserve.

The reason for good planning is that without a clear plan and an interesting lesson you might just as well give up – the pupils will not learn anything and will behave worse. You will soon come to hate every minute of being in the classroom. There is nothing more frightening than being in front of a class full of teenagers having badly misjudged how long your lesson will take and with nothing to hold their attention for the twenty minutes until the bell goes. Those experienced teachers who seem to take such short cuts have a wide repertoire of techniques and approaches in their heads that they have acquired and honed over the years. They used to write detailed lesson plans too. Their apparent nonchalance is evidence of many years of experience and careful planning. One day that will be you.

This chapter aims to set out a generic method of planning lessons so that it is not too time-consuming or onerous a task but that is realistic and allows for creativity on your

---

Suggested lesson structure
Timings should be roughly as follows:

- 10–15 minute settling, registration and introduction (Starter)
- 40–45 minute main lesson (introduction and development) (Main Course)
- 5 minute conclusion (Plenary)

Figure 3.1 Suggested lesson structure

part. It assumes lessons of one hour, but the ideas set out here are easily adjustable to work within other timeframes. Figure 3.1 outlines approximate timings for the sections of lessons. This is in an ideal world, of course. The classroom can be an unpredictable place, and so it will often be necessary for you to work flexibly with timing.

AIMS AND OBJECTIVES

To start with, you need to know what you are teaching, why you are teaching it and what you expect the pupils to learn in your lesson. Sometimes the first two parts of this are answered by the NC, the syllabus you are teaching, or by your department's Scheme of Work, but the specifics of the learning you wish to take place in the lesson you are about to teach are your responsibility.

First some definitions. The *aim* of the lesson is where you want to get to by the end; the *objectives* are the learning experiences you wish pupils to have along the way. So an aim might be 'To read through chapter 18' and the associated learning objectives could be 'To understand the author's use of figurative language and use these techniques in your own writing'. Schools usually have their own ways of expressing these, and they are often shared with pupils on the board. However, some useful ways of expressing your objectives are:

- By the end of the lesson you will know that . . . (for factual information).
- By the end of the lesson you will understand why . . . (for concepts).
- By the end of the lesson you will be able to . . . (for skills or analysis).
- By the end of the lesson you will be aware of . . . (for attitudes).

The sharing of your objectives will enable pupils to know what they are going to do, though there may be occasions where you will wish the pupils to set their own objectives for learning, or where you may deliberately wish to withhold your objectives. It is also a good idea to have learning outcomes in 'pupil friendly' language on the board. These will give the pupils a means by which to measure how successfully they have engaged with learning. Useful stems for these are:

- What I am looking for is . . .
- What I expect from everyone is . . .
- To be successful you will need to . . .
- By the end of the lesson, all of you will be able to . . . /most of you will be able to . . . /some of you will be able to . . .

The sharing and discussion of aims, objectives and outcomes seeks to ensure that all pupils know what they are learning and why, how to get it right and what success looks like. There is always a danger that the sharing of objectives can become a routine and meaning-less activity, though, so experiment with other methods. Challenging or provocative questions often provide a good way in. For example, if teaching *Much Ado About Nothing*: 'Who would you rather date, Benedick or Claudio and why?' or 'Who is Beatrice and what is she like?'

Planning for behaviour

'Teachers are now called upon to work with more and more [pupils] with more and more problems' (Canter and Canter, 2001).

Pupils need to know:

- What teachers expect of them.
- What will happen if they choose not to comply.
- How to choose responsible behaviour.

There are individuals and classes that are very challenging and some that are a constant drain on our energies. After you have taught these sorts of classes once or twice, you will have an idea of what to expect and so you can plan for behaviour. Sometimes we bypass the 'think' stage so that we are driven by what we feel. This means we are more reactive. Effective classroom management is more proactive and assertive. Planning for behaviour helps you to feel confident, puts you back in charge and settles the class down.

- Enlist the help of your mentor or Head of Department so that you have their support. Knowing that someone is standing by will give you confidence.
- Rule out activities such as cutting and sticking for a while.
- Short, sharply focused activities with a recognisable outcome work well; a quiz, reading a passage and answering questions on it in writing, individual work of all kinds.
- Do not attempt group work unless you are in control of the class. If you are unlucky enough to have a class clown, do not give them a platform.
- Reading a novel or a short story in 20 minute bursts is calming and disciplined.
- Tests and timed essays give everyone time off and allow those who want to work (always the majority) a chance to do so.

Avoid:

- Closed choices.
- The broken record.
- Power struggles.
- Getting sucked into dealing with secondary behaviour.

THREE-PART LESSONS

The three-part lesson is now a fairly standard form, related to the time structure in Figure 3.1. There follows a description of each part and some hints and tips on planning each section. Before beginning the formal lesson, however, the class must enter the room, settle down and the register be called. The aim is to get the pupils into the classroom, registered, occupied and thinking rather than discussing the weekend or last night's telly. You could try getting the pupils to answer the register in a way that corresponds to your lesson – to answer with a Shakespearean insult, or an adjective to describe themselves (more fun is to make it alliterative with their name), for instance. This is quick, gets them listening to each other and sets the tone for the lesson. This technique works best when it is used sparingly, otherwise it loses its novelty value.

The starter

This should last between five and ten minutes; however, it is easy for a starter to run and run, expanding to fill a large part of the lesson, or for it to die out within a couple of minutes. Neither of these situations is good, as the intention of the starter is to pave the way for the main fare of the lesson. It is a good idea to have the starter up on the whiteboard as they come in, so they can see at once what they have to do. Alternatively, try quick-fire, no-hands-up questions on the topic of the lesson, or something physical – 'Simon Says' could work well before a lesson on writing to instruct, for example. You could ask for a written response on mini-whiteboards that they can then show you. There are dozens of things that you can do for a starter, so ask around in your department for ideas. The starter should be a quick and thought-provoking activity that relates closely to the main focus of the lesson or that addresses an important and generally applicable skill (e.g. punctuation, homophones and homonyms or spelling patterns).

Lesson planning commentary

Class: Year 9 mixed ability.

Scheme of Work: Improving Writing. I have arrived at the 'writing to entertain and imagine' section. We have done 2 lessons on narrative perspectives so now they know the difference between first and third person narratives and many of them know what an omniscient narrator is. The obvious outcome of this section of the scheme of work is story writing. I am concerned with the dull openings for stories that they write. The department has a useful list of narrative hooks, but I want them to try writing in short bursts – 'flash fiction'. I need a learning objective as a focus for the single lesson. What do I really want them to learn? *LO = Analysing what makes a good opening and applying this to my own writing.*

I am sure they tell each other stories (mostly gossip) all the time, so I will tap into this for my starter.

Starter: (5 mins) Tell someone next to you something you know but they don't; an anecdote or little story. Followed by – what made you want to listen? What were the opening words? What grabs your attention? (Some class sharing here.)

Development:

- (10 mins) Prepared opening sentences from short stories on strips of paper. Stick at the top of an A4 piece of paper. Write the next sentence and pass around 3 or 4 times. (I'll judge how many times from the way it's going).
- (5 mins) Get your original back. What words/punctuation/ideas in it gave an idea of what was to follow? Which, out of the 3 or 4 you saw, was a good opening sentence? Why? (Discussion).
- (15 mins) Moving on to opening paragraphs. Model the annotation of an opening paragraph on the whiteboard. They have paragraphs in the middle of an A4 piece of paper. They annotate. Checklist up my sleeve for the less able.
- (15 mins) Having had these models, I am confident that they know what to do. The sheet on "narrative hooks" comes into play. They choose one, write for 5 mins and give it to their neighbour. I have the Teachit timer on the board. The neighbour annotates the paragraph in the same way as they did the one I gave them.

I now think that they have a good grasp of what makes a good opening and are able to apply this to their own writing.

Plenary: (5 mins) To make sure the quality of the paragraphs is good, I get some of them to read their opening out with as much drama as they can. [In later lessons they will go on to write a recipe for a good opening, to consider how to create tension and finally to write their own stories (I have to decide whether to let them pick their own genre or to use a murder mystery scheme). What I am sure is that their writing has improved.]

The main course

This is the main business of teaching and learning. This is what you wanted to do when you started teaching and may still be doing in twenty years' time. As you grow in experience you will experiment with a wide repertoire of approaches and you will sometimes (often?) get it wrong and teach lessons that do not go well. When it goes right though, there is nothing like it. You may even catch yourself thinking that it is so exhilarating you would do this job for free.

The introduction

This is where you lay out the business of the lesson. The topic or the text; whatever it is, the pupils should be clear as to what they are going to be doing and learning. You need confidence to pull this off and convince them that they want to learn what you have to teach, so droning at them isn't going to work. Be energetic and enthusiastic even if you do not feel it. They have to believe that there is nothing else you would rather be doing right at that moment than teaching them the thing you are. Think of imaginative ways in to the topic, read a tantalising extract, show a film clip, listen to some music, explore some pictures, or try a puzzle. The introduction (a few minutes to a quarter of an hour) should introduce pupils to the ideas and issues they need to progress into the next section.

Development

This section of the lesson is about activity related to and applying the material of the introduction. It is where the pupils explore initial learning. This may be an individual, paired or group activity, structured carefully by you. They could do some text-marking, for instance, or make a list of points for and against having a character from *Of Mice and Men* thrown out of a balloon. Careful thinking about time is also important. Countdown timers are readily available, or you can look at the clock, but remember you are in charge. Giving pupils time instructions and reminders ('five minutes to go') helps them to manage their work. Be sensitive, though; if they need more time, give it to them in measured amounts so that tasks can be completed well. Do not wait for the last slowcoach to finish, though, as they may need to learn to speed up.

When you want the pupils to finish, draw them back as a whole class to re-focus on the lesson objectives and to set up the next activity, which should be different from the first and should build upon it. Perhaps pairs could join up into fours, or perhaps it is the time to get them to make notes or plan an essay. Home and expert groups are particularly useful when planning essays or revising a topic. The class is divided into 'home' groups; these are the people for whom each group member will be gathering different information. Each member of the home group is given a number (1–5, say). All the 5s then go into a group, all the 4s and so on. They then become 'expert' on one aspect of the topic. At the end of an agreed time, the expert groups break up, return to the home groups and feed back their information. It is a motivating and satisfying way of covering a wide range of material in the lesson. If you are improvising some drama, it is showtime!

The end of this time is a good moment to set homework, which will usually build upon the work done in this section of the lesson. This also avoids the setting of homework becoming a rushed and poorly understood event as the class is packing away and leaving.

The plenary

We have all been to conferences and training where the dreaded plenary is timetabled and we look at our watches wondering if we could slip out before it to catch the early train. I sometimes feel that if I were 14 and had to endure five or six plenaries a day, it might all become too much. Of course, as the teacher, you have to run four or five or even six plenaries a day so you owe it to yourself and to the pupils not to be dull.

The best way to have a successful plenary is to blend it seamlessly into the lesson. You could make pupils' feedback on the main lesson activity the plenary; they could read their best sentences out, or try and catch the rest of the class out with a question based on the lesson. You could give them a five-question quiz with 1000 points per right answer (even Year 11s will enjoy that one) or do something clever with the mini-whiteboards. Depending on the way you have phrased your learning aims and objectives, you can return to them in the form of a question – 'Show me or show your neighbour what you have learned about . . .' It is a way of demonstrating to them what they have learned and for you to assess whether they have fulfilled the aims and objectives. If you send them off knowing what they have learned, feeling that they have made progress and that the lesson has gone quickly, you are onto a winner next time you see them. Simply asking pupils what they have learned, however, often elicits little useful information, just a litany of learning objectives being read back to you.

Activity 3.1

A sequence of activities to enhance your planning skills

a) Take a poem for teaching at either KS3 or KS4.

b) Read it through, annotating it for meaning and for the poet's use of language.

c) Now you know what you want the pupils to learn about it. Formulate your *learning objectives* in a clear and concise way. For a poem there are always two aims; meaning and the way form relates to meaning. The second is obviously much harder for pupils to grasp. You may have a third: to compare this poem with others. Look at the stems for phrasing the objectives above and formulate a snappy yet clear objective or two. Bear the plenary in mind as you may want to return to the objectives.

d) *The starter:* think about the ways in which pupils could relate to the poem. They could write a secret paragraph about the way they really feel about their siblings ('Sister Maude'). They could compile a class list of places for a romantic weekend ('In Paris with You'). You could compile a 'Call My Bluff' quiz based on difficult vocabulary in the poem. The list goes on . . .

e) *Introduction and the main part of the lesson:* How will you get them to read the poem? Will you do it? Will they read to each other? Round the class? Or to themselves? It is good to vary it from lesson to lesson, but it is important to plan for multiple readings to allow pupils to understand it properly. The main decision here is whether you are going to tell the pupils about the poem, whether they are to explore it for themselves (perhaps in discussion with a partner), or a mixture of both. You know what you

---

Activity 4.3 *continued*

want them to learn, to annotate and to make notes about and you need to think about how this can happen most effectively. You may, for example, want some creative writing (What happens after the envoy leaves the Duke's palace in 'My Last Duchess'? Or what incident turned Medusa into the 'Medusa' of Duffy's poem? Or what does Sister Maude's sister say in her dramatic monologue?) in the lesson or for homework. Be creative and take some risks; it is more fun for them and more exciting for you. There should be one or two different types of activity during the lesson. Think about your resources and what you could do with them (a colleague of mine had a great lesson with her AS class writing quotations about characters on strips of paper and making paper chains; the longest chain got a prize.) Mini-whiteboards, worksheets, drama, scissors and glue – anything to engage them and make them remember the lesson.

f) *Plenary:* find out whether they have fulfilled your learning objectives for the lesson. Decide whether they are going to hold up their annotated poem or whether you're going to have a Q and A with 'no hands up' or something else. This bit is for you to assess whether you need to do some more on this poem next lesson or whether they have got it!

POSSIBLE PITFALLS

Getting your timings wrong

This is why you have to set out your plans with each activity carefully timed when you are a beginning teacher; there is nothing worse than getting this wrong. Either you are left for the last ten minutes of a lesson looking desperately at the clock as the class becomes restive and crowds round the door, or the bell goes just as you are in the middle of explaining something and a mad rush to get out ensues as the next class bundles in.

It is better to have too much rather than too little. Keep one activity up your sleeve in case the class finish sooner than you thought they would. Similarly, be prepared to cut down on time or a whole activity if they are being slow. This really is a matter of experience. Established teachers do not get it right all the time. Just remember that it takes less than a minute for Years 9–11 to pack away and ages for Year 7s to even pick up a pair of scissors.

Forgetting equipment

You really shouldn't leave your class to go and photocopy a worksheet, find a set of textbooks or hunt for a memory stick. Write a list of resources in your planner and check before the lesson to make sure you have everything. If you need mini-whiteboards and dry wipe pens, make sure they are in the classroom at break or lunchtime, make sure you know the password for the whiteboard and that your IWB pen works. Leave yourself photocopying time; there is bound to be a queue just when you want to use the machine. Above all, make sure you have paper and pens for those few in every class who do not have their books, pencil cases or any sense of remorse at having forgotten them. Arm yourself with detention slips and any other pieces of paper to do with discipline or allowing a pupil to the toilet or whatever, so you can deal with things smoothly and without interrupting the flow of your lesson.

Dealing with the unexpected

Having all your equipment and your fascinating lesson plan does not mean everything will go to plan. Schools are places where the unexpected is normal; fire drills, someone fainting, double bookings of the computer rooms, etc. There is no magic answer here. You just have to keep calm and do the best you can. Forward planning can help to some extent but living with the frustration of finding half of your class (and the nicer half at that) are out on a trip is just one of those things. Put it down to experience and remember that you can always do that fabulous lesson again next year.

Friday afternoon

It is true that almost anything is better than Year 9 on a Friday afternoon. Perhaps once in every ten years your timetable will have a free lesson on a Friday afternoon, so you will have to learn to deal with lessons that are difficult by virtue of the position on the timetable (like the lesson before lunch, Sports Day, the school talent show or other exciting events). Careful planning is really helpful at times like this. Your aim will be to have a peaceful and productive time. It is not the time to start new topics or do a lesson on melodrama complete with fake blood and plastic swords.

Planning checklist

Do you have:

- *Learning objectives* clear in your mind so that you can write them on the board?
- Your *timings* written down?
- *An alternative approach* involving quiet individual writing in case the planned discussion/drama work is scuppered by behavioural issues?
- An idea for *homework* if the timings are too mean?
- An *extension task* if the timings are too generous?
- *Equipment* (copies of the text/spare copies for those who have forgotten theirs; worksheets; spare pens, pencils, scissors, glue (etc.); whiteboard pens; DVDs/CDs; memory stick; mark book/planner with your lesson plan in it?
- *A calm and confident demeanour*, ready to greet the little darlings with a smile and a cheery word?

CONCLUSIONS

Planning lessons carefully and creatively will result in your pupils progressing in their learning. Having an interesting and challenging time in class can help with several classroom management issues. Then too, your job will be much more absorbing, fulfilling and enjoyable. In a few years' time you will be in the same position as those experienced teachers in the staffroom who seem to plan on the way downstairs to their classrooms, teach lively and popular lessons and still have time in the evenings to have a life.

RECOMMENDED READING

Canter, L. and Canter, M. (2001) *Assertive Discipline: Positive Behavior Management for Today's Classroom*. Third edition. Denver, CO: Canter & Associates.

Cohen, L., Manion, L. and Morrison, K. (2004) Beginning Curriculum Planning, in *A Guide to Teaching Practice*. Fifth edition. London: Routledge, pp. 124–64.

Davison, J. and Leask, M. (2009) Schemes of Work and Lesson Planning, in S. Capel, M. Leask and T. Turner (eds) *Learning to Teach in the Secondary School*. Fifth edition. London: Routledge, pp. 79–90.

Leask, M. and Watts, M. (2009) Taking Responsibility for Whole Lessons, in S. Capel, M. Leask and T. Turner (eds) *Learning to Teach in the Secondary School*. Fifth edition. London: Routledge, pp. 91–103.

McIntyre, J. and Green, A. (2011) Planning the Curriculum, in A. Green (ed.) (2011) *Becoming a Reflective English Teacher*. Maidenhead: Open University Press, pp. 43–57.

Chapter 4   Teaching writing

ANDREW GREEN

In this chapter you will consider:

- your personal views of writing;
- what you understand by writing;
- collaborative writing;
- talk for writing;
- barriers to effective writing;
- how to support writing;
- how to generate content for writing.

INTRODUCTION

Contrary to popular belief (a belief often reinforced by the media and politicians) many of the pupils you teach are frequent writers. For you as a teacher of English, struggling hard to encourage your classes to write very much (or even anything at all), this may seem hard to believe. But from morning to night your pupils will be writing – texting, emailing, on social media sites, on gaming forums of different kinds. Such kinds of writing are often forgotten about or dismissed, or even blamed for falling standards in the formal, educational writing pupils are expected to do at school. However, as teachers of English, to overlook and damn this kind of writing would be an error. Of course – and quite rightly – pupils need to be taught the requirements and forms of analytical writing, of report writing, of creative writing in a variety of forms, and so on. It is important to recognise, however, that if we are to enthuse our pupils as writers and enable them to feel empowered as creators of text, we need to acknowledge, utilise and build upon the writing forms that they freely and confidently engage with. To do otherwise would be to undermine pupils at the very point where we need to be building them up.

Activity 4.1

Testing texting

Much is said about the influence of texting and text language on pupils' writing. But what do we really know? Text language actually requires quite high levels of

> ### Activity 4.1 *continued*
>
> language awareness (surrounding omitted vowels, for instance, and phonics (e.g. gr8 = great; 2 = to), and text language functions perfectly grammatically).
>
> Test it out. How are you going to demonstrate if and how text talk is a significant influencing factor on writing as opposed to, say, watching *Eastenders* or listening to NDubz? There are too many variables in the pupils' language biographies to isolate one factor as the defining influence on their written language without further testing.
>
> Try setting up a specific test – set a writing task, requiring half the class to prepare their work in a conventional form of school language and the other half to prepare using text language. Both groups are then to produce their final piece of work in Standard English. Then analyse closely whether or not there are identifiable trends within these two groups. Do the texters write better or worse than the others? You could replicate this test across a range of groups and for a range of purposes to see whether there are generalisable outcomes.

Perhaps part of the difficulty here is that writing is so often seen as a high stakes means of assessment. Pupils are drilled in the formulas of PEE (point, evidence, explanation), FLAP (form, language, audience, purpose) in ways that risk constricting their sense of the possibilities of writing variation. The desire to play with words and to create new ways of conveying meaning can be lost as pupils come to believe there is a formulaic, right way to write. Writing can all too easily become an uninspiring pursuit of formula rather than a creatively personal medium of expression. This is said, of course, not to denigrate the need for pupils to learn appropriate forms of writing, but to observe that an overzealous application of form and method can have undesirable impact on pupils' writing.

The purpose of this chapter is to consider a range of ways in which we can support and develop pupils' writing without falling into the traps identified above. By employing a range of approaches to teaching writing – including using the forms of writing pupils readily engage with (why for example should note-making not be in text language?) – and encouraging pupils to see writing as provisional and exploratory, not simply as final product, we can create classrooms where writing generates enthusiasm rather than confrontation and groans.

PERSONAL VIEWS OF WRITING

To begin with, it is important to think about your personal understanding of and views of writing. What, as a beginning teacher in English, are your perceptions of the writing pupils do in the secondary school? It is important to capture your initial views of what pupils do when they write, as these will inevitably have a significant impact upon the ways in which you will set about the teaching of writing.

> ### Activity 4.2
>
> #### Pupils' writing
>
> Think carefully about the following questions and jot down your responses.
>
> - What is writing?
> - What are the features of writing?

Activity 4.2 *continued*

- Why is it that children find it hard to develop the composition of their writing?
- What skills and understanding do children need to possess in order to develop the composition of their writing?
- What support do children need in order to develop compositional writing?
- Who do pupils write for?

It is also very important to think about yourself as a writer. Do you write regularly yourself? Do you enjoy writing or do you do it on sufferance? What kinds of writing do you do? Are you a good or indifferent speller? Do you feel confident in the grammatical construction of your writing? What about possessive apostrophes? Do you like to plan meticulously before committing yourself to paper, or do you prefer to pitch straight in and see how a piece of writing emerges in a more organic way? What are your processes as a writer? Do you like or dislike redrafting your writing? How confident are you in your abilities as a writer? All these questions are just as relevant to you as a teacher of writing as they are to your pupils, and they will impact upon the confidence with which you approach teaching writing. To help you shape your views and understanding further, see Activity 4.2.

Activity 4.3

What is writing about?

Consider each of the following quotations about writing. What does each of them suggest about the activity of writing? Which comes nearest to your own views of writing?

1   Fetch me a pen, I need to think. (Voltaire)
2   There's nothing to writing. All you do is sit down at a typewriter and open a vein. (Walter Wellesley "Red" Smith)
3   Writing became such a process of discovery that I couldn't wait to get to work in the morning: I wanted to know what I was going to say. (Sharon O'Brien)
4   I'm not a very good writer, but I'm an excellent rewriter. (James Michener)
5   Easy reading is damn hard writing. (Nathaniel Hawthorne)
6   The difference between the right word and the almost right word is the difference between lightning and a lightning bug. (Mark Twain)
7   Write down the thoughts of the moment. Those that come unsought for are commonly the most valuable. (Francis Bacon)
8   Write your first draft with your heart. Re-write with your head. (From the movie *Finding Forrester*)
9   How do I know what I think until I see what I say? (E. M. Forster)

WHAT DO YOU UNDERSTAND BY WRITING?

This may, at first seem rather a simplistic question. Writing is writing, you may feel. However, in reality the answer to this question is not so straightforward. The American novelist Truman Capote memorably dismissed the work of his compatriot Jack Kerouac:

'That's not writing, that's typing!' The remark is clearly flippant, perhaps derived from personal rivalry, but it serves to illustrate the point that writing has both qualitative and quantitative dimensions. Perhaps it also helps if we understand that Kerouac used to type his manuscripts on to huge rolls of paper so he never had to stop work to change a sheet of paper. So writing has to do with means of production as well as content produced.

Such issues are very relevant to your thinking about writing as a teacher of English. Nowadays we live and work in a world where we rarely write by hand, word processing instead, on to a variety of electronic devices. Such changes in technology lead to fundamentally different writing processes and ways of constructing and presenting written text. This raises many issues for the teacher of English. How do we enable pupils to produce a range of effective writing across a spectrum of contexts and employing multiple means of textual production (pen, word processor, hand-held devices, etc.)? It is important that pupils are introduced to a variety of ways of conceiving the act of writing so that they are enabled to function as writers in multiple contexts and for a plurality of purposes. Conventional handwritten text is still a part of this picture, but is by no means all of it.

Let us think also about forms of writing. The NC identifies a wide range of forms of writing that pupils are expected to approach both as receivers (readers) and producers (writers). To name but a few of the text types covered within the subject orders, there is prose fiction, prose non-fiction, lyric poetry, narrative poetry, information writing, scripts of various kinds (e.g. stage, radio, television, film) and multimodal texts. Then there are such forms as web text, blogging and texting. All of these types of writing have their own demands and specific features, and all make different demands of the writer (and associated reader or audience).

The NC breaks writing as an activity down into a range of purposes, known as the triplets:

- to argue, persuade, advise;
- to analyse, review, comment;
- to explore, imagine, entertain;
- to inform, explain, describe.

These are inevitably somewhat false distinctions, and there are significant areas of crossover between them. When we seek to persuade, for instance, we will also frequently describe, analyse and explore. Likewise, when we write to argue we will frequently entertain, comment and inform. However, there are useful distinctions to be made in relation to each of these purposes for writing (e.g. the use of imperative verb forms in writing to advise, or the use of figurative language in writing to describe). Each also implies a different stance on what writing is, and it is important to think carefully about how writing looks different in each of these guises.

We may rightly question whether writing even necessarily involves the physical action of transferring words on to paper or screen (whether using a pen or a word processor). When we tell stories, are we not involved in an act of textual composition, and therefore writing? Oral 'text' is an important part of the world of words. This does not mean that all spoken word can (or should) be seen as writing, but there are significant areas of crossover between the spoken word and the written word. Spoken language frequently becomes part of written text in the form of reported dialogue (either as direct or indirect speech) in newspapers, for instance. Stylised spoken language in the form of novelistic dialogue and scripted speech for drama, film or television is oral 'text'. Speeches and television broadcasts are forms of text more usually heard than read, but they are also forms of composed or written text.

All of these examples demonstrate that as a teacher of English you need to think very carefully about what actually constitutes writing, the range of purposes to which it is put in the secondary English classroom and how you will approach this.

Activity 4.4

Reconceiving writing

How does this make you think differently about what writing actually is?

How might you approach some of these complex issues with classes at KS3, KS4 and post-16?

TALK FOR WRITING

Writing is often seen as a solitary experience. Such a view is no doubt encouraged by a cultural view (often unfounded, as the acknowledgements pages of countless literary works testify) of the writer as a tortured lonely genius. In reality, however, while elements of written composition require undistracted individual work, large parts of the process of writing provide the possibility for (and thrive upon) collaborative work. Do not feel, therefore, that writing in class should always be done in silence. Reserve silence for when it really matters and when it is genuinely beneficial.

Writing, as suggested above, benefits from collaboration. Sharing ideas, talking about possibilities as a means of generating or developing content for writing, testing out choices of language and their impact upon readers, exploring dimensions of 'voice' and tone, providing critical feedback and discussing compositional process are all very important in helping pupils to develop as writers. These and other opportunities for pupils to engage in talk for writing should be planned for and encouraged. By developing appropriate forums for talking about writing, teachers can generate enthusiasm for the process, can ensure that pupils have discussed in some detail the content, form and purpose of their writing, and as such are well prepared for the moment when they do indeed need to sit down alone and write. By allowing these discussions to take place 'externally' and by structuring them carefully, pupils will learn more and more to internalise these dialogues, thus making them more genuinely independent and autonomous writers.

A very effective way of approaching this kind of work is an approach known as shared writing. As its name suggests, shared writing is collaborative in nature and brings with it particular benefits for pupils in their learning of writing:

- Its structure helps pupils appreciate the importance of planning, drafting and editing writing.
- It provides a teacher-led model of how an effective writing process works.
- It provides an opportunity for writers of a wide range of abilities to write in non-threatening collaboration.
- It encourages mutual sharing of ideas.
- The process of working together on a shared written outcome allows for self- and peer-assessment.
- The lack of individual exposure as pupils experiment with new writing skills enhances confidence to take risks.
- It provides a forum for teacher and pupils to collaborate on a piece of writing to challenge and extend writing skills.
- The teacher, a Learning Support Assistant (or a more able pupil if appropriate) can model aspects of writing using the pupils' suggestions.
- Focus upon a range of elements of writing is possible – e.g. structure, content, revision and improvement.
- Writing can be closely linked to reading.

Talk about the writing is clearly integral to this process. Text and textual production become the focus of teacher-led dialogue, allowing pupils to explore in a guided and carefully structured activity the nuances of content, language and process.

Activity 4.5

Shared writing

If working with a group of pupils, the shared writing activity outlined below would clearly require differentiated support, but it will give some insight into the kinds of processes you might employ. If possible, gather together with other beginning teachers of English to work through this sequence.

- Read Charles Dickens' account of Scrooge's return to his house in the first Stave of *A Christmas Carol*.
- Look closely at how Dickens uses dialogue, language, variation in sentence length and pace to create a sense of fear and suspense.
- Write your own paragraph or sequence of paragraphs describing a building, creating an atmosphere of fear.
- Decide on one of the paragraphs that you will use to work on as the basis for a piece of shared writing.
- Select one person to act as 'teacher'.
- Collaborate on the piece, focussing on dialogue, language, variation in sentence length and pace to develop fear and suspense in the writing.

SUPPORTING WRITING

Many pupils find difficulty in developing the composition of their writing. This may be for a range of reasons, but some of the most significant are that they lack:

- first-hand experience as writers;
- reading models to refer to in order to help them structure their thoughts, make appropriate language selections, generate suitable content, etc.;
- the knowledge of and ability to employ the features of a given text type or genre;
- the means to plan their writing (individually, in small groups or as a whole class);
- triggers to promote composition;
- teachers who effectively intervene at the point of writing;
- incisive teacher feedback and target-setting during the writing process and once the writing has been completed.

It is very important, therefore, that you think carefully about how to provide suitable support to develop your pupils as writers. Figure 4.1 identifies a range of strategies you might employ to support weaker writers and their associated benefits and disadvantages.

A SEQUENCE FOR TEACHING WRITING

There is an understandable danger, alluded to earlier, that pupils tend to see writing as a finished product rather than as a developing process. It is important that we help pupils to understand that writing is a sequence of linked stages progressing towards a final version, and that even the most able writers have to work at their writing in order to hone

Strategy	Advantages	Disadvantages
Modelling and scaffolding: shared writing; supported composition	Provides insight into how text types function; non-threatening, collaborative work	If scaffolding is not steadily removed, pupils can become over-dependent on support
Focusing on the writing process	Helps pupils to think 'beyond the moment'; helps them to see that writing is a developmental, iterative process	Can be abstract or invisible if not carefully explained
Writing for real audiences	Provides exciting 'real' purpose for writing; incentive for quality	What will be the response (if any) to the pupils' writing; this may be disheartening if not carefully managed
Using children's experience	Pupils will often write best about things they have experienced	Pupils' experiences can sometimes be very limited and limiting
Writing frames	Provide an essential structure for writing and provide insight into how different text types function	If these are too rigid they can be limiting rather than liberating; overdependence on frames can hinder independence
Sentence starters	Provide pupils with a way in to writing; help pupils understand language constructions useful within text types	Can appear prescriptive and can limit creative alternative ways in
Triggers for composition: visuals; drama and role play; talk	Open up possible ways of looking at the world as a stimulus for writing	Can, if not carefully handled, close down creative alternatives
Ensuring that children understand and can use key features of text types	These help pupils structure and organise their writing appropriately and help them develop suitable language and content	Can become a quantitative 'checklist' (have I used enough devices) rather than a qualitative overview
Marking, feedback and target-setting	Provides insight into what pupils need to do to improve their work	Can make writing seem as if it is only for assessment – this can stunt enjoyment and risk-taking
In-class conferencing	Creates a varied range of contexts within which pupils can discuss their writing; could be drama focused (e.g. newsroom, editorial meeting) if desired	Requires careful planning and class management; criteria for success in writing need to be made clear
Writing/editing partners		
Providing a supportive and print-rich classroom environment, e.g. displayed texts as models for children's writing, word banks	Provides a range of relevant resources that pupils can access for themselves to support their work independent of the teacher	Resources must be updated regularly for relevance to task or text; high levels of accuracy required; time-intensive

Figure 4.1 Strategies for supporting writing

it. Figure 4.2 provides a useful overview of a process for teaching writing. It is worth observing that the central sections of this process (the drafting ⇨ editing ⇨ redrafting stages) may be completed on several occasions before progressing to the finished article.

Importantly, use and discussion of this kind of cycle provides pupils with an insight into how writers work. It helps them see that much writing is provisional rather than final and that it frequently involves taking risks and making mistakes. It should also serve to make them more aware of the possibilities available to them as writers and to think in more critical ways about the choices they make as creators of text. This kind of metacognitive awareness (Flavell, 1976) is an important dimension of learning as it requires pupils to think about the process of problem solving, to examine how they think and do things, to be aware of process, strategies and types of thought and how these can lead to differing outcomes, and ultimately to conscious application of procedure in a variety of situations (see Figure 4.3).

Using draft manuscripts by great authors (and ideally of texts the pupils are themselves studying) helps to illustrate the fact that even great writers have to work to hone their craft

Element	Function
Note-making	Gathering ideas; collecting useful words; annotating texts; brainstorming; spider diagram or mind-map.
Planning	Flow diagram of key points; paragraph plan; opening sentence.
Drafting	Turning ideas into sentences; turning sentences into paragraphs; experimenting.
Editing	Reading through, thinking about how effective the text is as a whole; making changes and corrections.
Redrafting	Making changes and corrections on a word processor or rewriting by hand, producing the final draft.
Checking	Reading through carefully, correcting any mistakes.

Figure 4.2 A process for teaching writing

Make decisions without thinking about them	tacit use
Conscious awareness of strategy or process	aware use
Select the best strategies for solving a problem	strategic use
Reflect on thinking before, during and after process, setting targets for improvement	reflective use

Figure 4.3 Levels of awareness (drawing on Flavell, 1976)

and that works of genius did not simply drop from their pens, as pupils often think. This also exemplifies process in writing, and can also be used to illustrate that writing, even at the highest level, is often a shared process. Newspaper journalists' work is subject to editorial control, not the work of a single hand, and literary works often rely on input from fellow authors.

The relationship between T. S. Eliot and Ezra Pound in the construction of the final manuscript for *The Waste Land* is a particularly famous example, and a full facsimile of the draft manuscript is readily available. Likewise, the young Wilfred Owen was indebted to the more established poet Siegfried Sassoon in the composition of his famous poem 'Anthem for Doomed Youth', which he wrote whilst being treated at Craiglockhart Hospital. The interaction of the two poets on the final manuscript is vividly recreated by Pat Barker in her novel *Regeneration*.

Much useful work can also be done with pupils in looking at the ways in which the poem changed between its original draft and final published versions. These are available at http://www.lancs.ac.uk/fass/projects/stylistics/topic1b/2anthem.htm. Draft versions of many well-known and frequently taught poems are easily available online.

Creative assessment: working with drafts

Try this activity out for yourself, using the poems at http://www.lancs.ac.uk/fass/ projects/stylistics/topic1b/2anthem.htm. This would also work very well with groups of pupils from KS3 through to post-16 level and beyond in encouraging them to think about the development of vocabulary (word level), syntax (sentence level) and structure (text level) choices in writing processes.

1   Look closely at the changes made by Owen in the course of drafting the poem and the replacement choices he made. Taking each example in turn, consider the choices he has made and discuss the impact of these on the reader.
2   Now compare the draft version to the final published version of the poem. In your groups, discuss which of the two versions of the poem you feel is better. You should explain any observations you make by detailed reference to the poem.
3   What insights does this exercise give you into the process of Owen's writing and the important role of others in developing writing in shared contexts?

STIMULATING WRITING

A range of exercises can be used to help pupils with finding ways into writing. Below are four ways in which you might seek to stimulate content for writing, along with a set of exercises you might try out for yourself and with a range of classes you teach. I have used these activities effectively, with appropriate levels of support and intervention, with pupils from KS2 right up to postgraduate students.

Using music

Music can be used to create and manipulate emotion, to create aural 'pictures', to create atmosphere, to evoke memory, to suggest narrative, etc. All of these can be very useful in creating starting points for writing.

Activity 4.7

Using music

- Listen to musical extracts creating a variety of moods. Classical or instrumental music works best, as lyrics add a layer of meaning of their own and as such tend to distract from the focus of the activity.
- A good range of musical extracts would be: the opening of *The Rite of Spring* (Stravinsky), the opening of Symphony No. 1 – 'The Gothic' (Havergal Brian), *Harlem* (Duke Ellington), *The Mississippi Suite* (Ferde Grofé), *The Planets Suite* (Gustav Holst).
- Listen to each extract once without writing anything. Allow the music to have its own effect on you.
- When the extract is played again, use your thoughts as the basis for a short paragraph. The focus of this could be descriptive, atmospheric or narrative.

Using pictures

Visual stimulus can also be useful for creating first thoughts about writing. Some writers, like William Blake and many children's authors, use pictures as an integral part of their writing.

Activity 4.8

Using pictures

Choose a picture of a person to be used as a stimulus. This could be either a painting or a photograph.

- What is the person's name?
- Think about their family and how they relate to them.
- Think about their friends and how they relate to them.
- Think about what they like doing.
- Where are they and why are they there?
- Brainstorm a selection of adjectives you'd use to describe this person.
- How do their clothes reflect their character?
- Write a paragraph introducing this character, using any details that you find effective.

Using physical objects

Physical objects are a very good way into writing, as they allow pupils to explore the sensory possibilities of objects (how they feel, smell, sound, look, etc.). This can provide interesting ways in to description, atmosphere and narrative possibilities.

Activity 4.9

Using objects

This will work best in a group, but can be undertaken individually.

- Each person selects an object from their bag or pocket. (Or these could be pre-selected and supplied by the teacher.)
- Each person now selects one object – not their own.
- Taking it in turns, use as many of the senses as you can to help you describe the object to your group. Take one minute each. Levels of challenge can be introduced as desired by proscribing the use of certain words (e.g. nice, heavy, smelly), which are too obvious or lazy as vocabulary choices.
- Now select three of the objects. Imagine each of these objects is going to play a significant part in a story. Explain what the role of each in the plot will be.

Using places

Using real places allows for a more holistic and personal engagement with a real place with all of its descriptive, atmospheric, sensory and narrative possibilities.

Activity 4.10

Using places

- Take your group to a particular place or, if possible, send them to a variety of places.
- Give pupils 10–15 minutes to write a description of this place.
- Levels of challenge can be increased by placing certain genre requirements on different individuals (e.g. how would this place be described differently if it were for use in a ghost story, a romance, a Harry Potter novel, a thriller, etc.).
- The pupils should then read their descriptions to each other and explain why they chose to describe this place in the way they did, and the rest of the group can give constructive feedback.

CONCLUSIONS

The teaching of writing is a complex and multi-faceted part of the English teacher's work. The forms of writing with which pupils are required to engage proliferate almost daily. Technological advances are constantly creating new media, new genres and with them come new implications for the nature and impact of writing. Thinking about what writing entails, therefore, and how to create effective balances between the types of writing pupils wish and need to engage with personally and those required of them by the formal education system is essential. Under these circumstances, it is more than ever important that teachers of English think deeply about the processes pupils need to develop in order to handle the developing demands of writing, and to enable pupils to be autonomous developers of their own writing.

RECOMMENDED READING

Andrews, R. (2011) A new theory and model of writing development, in J. Davison, C. Daly and J. Moss (eds) *Debates in English Teaching*. London: Routledge, pp. 48–62.

Flavell, J. H. (1976) Metacognitive aspects of problem solving, in L. B. Resnick (ed.) *The nature of intelligence*. Hillsdale, NJ: Erlbaum, pp. 231–6.

Fleming, M. and Stevens, D. (2004) Writing, in M. Fleming and D. Stevens, *English Teaching in the Secondary School*. London: David Fulton, pp. 77–92.

Green, A. (2004) Creative Writing, in R. Fisher and M. Williams (eds) *Unlocking Creativity*. London: David Fulton, pp. 37–54.

Moss, J. (2009) Writing, in J. Davison and J. Dowson (eds) *Learning to Teach English in the Secondary School*. London: Routledge, pp. 134–57.

Myhill, D. and Watson, A. (2011) Teaching Writing, in A. Green (ed.) *Becoming a Reflective English Teacher*. Maidenhead: McGraw-Hill, pp. 58–72.

Wilkinson, A. (1986) *The Quality of Writing*. Milton Keynes: Open University Press.

Chapter 5   **Drama in English**

ROB SMITH

In this chapter you will consider:

- the relationship between English and drama;
- your own experience and practice of drama in the English curriculum;
- practical ideas on how to use drama techniques in the English classroom;
- new ways of approaching texts to generate pupils' enthusiasm and strengthen their engagement.

INTRODUCTION

As a beginning teacher of English the thought of tackling drama in your own classroom may be daunting, particularly if you work in a school where drama exists as a discrete subject, taught in custom-built drama studios by specialist drama practitioners. You may be a capable teacher of drama in your own right but, equally, there are many teachers of English who can be apprehensive about how to fit drama into their schemes of work and how to tackle it given the fundamental physical restrictions of their classrooms. Whilst drama is an integral part of the English curriculum drama and English also have their own distinct and separate content which can lead to an uneasy relationship between the two. Take heart! This chapter aims to reconcile these tensions by considering practical, manageable ideas about how to approach English using drama techniques in the classroom, techniques which could also enliven pupils' interest and galvanise their enthusiasm.

VIEWS OF DRAMA

Drama is often a part of the secondary curriculum that is independent of English (taught and examined separately at GCSE and A Level). However, the NC in 1989 clearly placed drama within the Orders for English (within the Programme of Study for S&L) and it has remained there ever since. This strengthens a connection between drama and English that was highlighted in the Cox Report (1989). Although Cox made explicit the link between drama and language development, it is also the case that the English literary curriculum is full of set or recommended drama texts as well as novels and poems which are ripe with potential for exploration through the dramatic process.

Activity 5.1

Views of drama

- What are your views about the position of drama in English as set out in the NC (DCSF/QCA, 2007)?
- How far do you agree with the stance taken by the KS3 National Strategy Framework (DfEE, 2001) that drama objectives should sit within the lists of Speaking and Listening objectives?
- In the more recent publication: *The National Strategies Secondary: Developing Drama in English* (DfE, 2010) there is an attempt to embed drama more broadly across the wider domains of English (reading and writing besides S&L). What do you think about the changing attitude towards drama?

The aim of this chapter is to provide an overview of some of the possibilities of using drama in English. Before you begin, it might be valuable for you to reflect on your own experience of, and exposure to, drama throughout your time in education. Activity 5.2 will help you in this.

Activity 5.2

Personal experiences of drama

- Before you begin working through this chapter, make an audit of your own experience of drama.
- What do you remember of drama in the English classroom in which you worked as a secondary school pupil?
- Did you participate in drama beyond the English classroom? School plays? Theatre visits? Or . . .?
- What kind of drama 'training' have you experienced in preparation for your role as a teacher?
- Reflect carefully on your own teaching styles, the ways in which your pupils learn and the range of groups you teach. Extend your reflection to encompass the pressures and demands of external assessment. Then fill out the table at Figure 5.1. What kind of balance results?

What do I think about using drama in my own classroom?	
FOR	**AGAINST**

Figure 5.1 Views of drama

Often, English is taught in fairly standard classrooms, densely filled with tables and chairs sufficient in number to accommodate large groups of pupils. To this end, many of the activities have been selected because they can work successfully in a small space such as a quickly adapted classroom and do not require specialist facilities or equipment. Furniture can be moved to the edges, circles of chairs positioned, or a small space cleared within or at the front of the room. It is even possible to use corridor or outdoor space with agreement from other staff. Remember that using drama is a way into texts of all genres, not just dramatic scripts and that drama activities can arise naturally within English lessons rather than requiring specialist planning and provision.

Activity 5.3

Accommodating drama

Think about your own classroom or a room in which you teach English regularly. Imagine how you could successfully adapt its layout to accommodate drama activities. Are there any potential problems with the physical landscape of your room which you might need to overcome?

BEGINNING DRAMA

It has always been seen as good practice to begin drama sessions or activities with a *warm up*. This can be extremely valuable as a way of physically preparing pupils for the active work that is to follow (it may even act as a safeguard against physical injury). It also signals clearly to pupils that they are likely to be undertaking a very different type of work. Perhaps the most important rationale, however, is the way in which warm up routines help to build confidence, trust, collaboration and group identity. Many drama games place an emphasis on a shared group goal; this is often a completely different experience for pupils who are used to being competitive. Finally, this type of activity invariably energises pupils' creative thinking and imagination and reduces inhibition and self-consciousness.

Since many classrooms are set up in a way that reinforces power or control structures (for example, teacher at the front, pupils in rows), *circle routines* are very effective in establishing neutrality.

1   Whilst sitting (or standing) in a circle, pupils can be encouraged to listen carefully to each other and operate within a 'group'. An ice-breaker (sometimes called 'Jack to Jill') involves one person speaking her/his name aloud and identifying another person in the circle, moving across to take her/his place. The process continues until all pupils have been involved. Instead of moving across the circle, pupils could throw a soft ball to each other.
2   The circle game 'I noticed . . .' encourages each pupil in turn to complete a sentence about what they noticed about their experience that day, about a text they have just started, about a film they have seen, or . . .?
3   You can make some of these activities incrementally challenging. For example, one game might be based on supplying missing adjectives: '*Macbeth* is a _____ play'. Perhaps you could then ask pupils to generate adjectives in alphabetical order.
4   Even a familiar game like 'I went to the supermarket and bought . . .' is a powerful routine. Each person decides on an object to 'buy' at the supermarket and when their turn comes they speak it aloud. However, they also have to remember and speak aloud the objects selected by all the pupils before them in the correct sequence. Whoever starts the list clearly has the easiest job but many pupils enjoy the challenge

of remembering everyone else's choices and they come up with clever mnemonic strategies to help recall.

5   Sometimes, encouraging pupil reflection and sharing of their thoughts is useful in order to create trust and respect. Select from a pack of 'States of Mind' cards (for example; 'Happiness', 'Relief', 'Confusion', etc.), distribute individually to pupils and ask them to articulate their thoughts about when they felt this way. After any of these activities you can have a period of reflection with the pupils. A powerful and effective way of encouraging them to listen carefully and take turns in speaking is to give them an object to hold as they speak. This is passed in turn to each speaker.

6   Follow Me: You (as teacher) stand at the front of the class and explain that you will perform a series of actions. Pupils copy the actions as you do them. Speed up to make the activity more challenging. Or ask the pupils to perform the action you did three or four moves before. Layer on language or textual references by asking the pupils to speak specific words as they move (for example, names of characters or locations associated with a particular text). As they become more confident, you could tackle a whole speech this way with you, the teacher, leading pupils through a soliloquy from a play you are studying.

7   Make a machine (or animal). In groups of four or five, pupils make a fully functioning machine or a moving animal. Their choices can be invented or 'real'. In the latter case, other pupils could be asked to guess what the machine or animal is.

Activity 5.4

Circle routines

- Focus on the previous section. Reflect on how some of these activities might fit (or be adapted to) the classroom context in which you work.
- As an extension to Activity 5.3, now draw some plans of your own classroom which show how you could reconfigure the layout to facilitate one of the warm up or circle routines.
- Argue the case for and against using circle routines in your lessons as a strategy for enhancing learning.
- Think about one of your teaching groups and a drama text that forms part of their Programme of Study. Find from it a developed speech by one character (this could be a soliloquy or a monologue). Plan a 'Follow me' routine in which you will lead your pupils through an active interpretation of the speech, fitting actions and gestures to the choral speaking of the script.

WORKING WITH TEXT: THE EARLY STAGES

Either give out to pupils, or let them collect for themselves, snatches of language from a text. Often it is useful to categorise these as 'sense units' (i.e. a sequence of words that makes sense when taken out of context). Write these on cards and distribute them at random. Pupils walk around the classroom speaking their text aloud and, at the same time, try to 'collect' as much language as possible from other pupils by listening to them speaking. This works particularly well in a darkened room. At the end of the exercise, ask pupils to write down any key words they have overheard. This word bank can be used for creative writing or for discussion. It is a really interesting way into a new text as the extracts can be manipulated in order to target ideas/themes/images central to the text.

Use the card extracts as the basis for improvised drama. In small groups, pupils can generate a short scene from the text on their cards. You can control this as much as you like, by, for example, insisting that all the language on the cards must be used, that all pupils have a speaking role and so on.

Activity 5.5

Language extracts

Choose a text that you are about to work on with a particular year group. Collect from it enough language extracts to fill out cards for each of the pupils in the group. Plan how you will use them as a springboard into one of the activities outlined above.

GROUP WORK: GETTING INTO GROUPS

Sometimes you will want to control the formation of pupil groupings. At other times it can be exciting if pupils work in new or fresh formations. In the latter case try this. Collect images of the front cover of four or five different editions of the book you are studying. Cut these up into jigsaw shapes and give each pupil one piece at random. They need to re-assemble the pictures (thereby forming a working group of pupils) and then discuss their images. You can do this with symbolic pictures, snaps of characters and so on.

STILL IMAGE OR TABLEAU

These can be used in many different ways. A tableau is like a sculpture or a still photograph, catching the presentation of a moment frozen in time. Still images can capture a key moment in a text, can fix a particular gesture, expression or movement. They can move beyond the text to record an incident that the text does not cover (for example, a scene ten years later). They might be highly planned and rehearsed to show off the nuances of particular relationships between characters or they might be used to 'freeze-frame' a moment in a dynamic action sequence (a 'snapshot' at the height of a riot between the Montagues and the Capulets, for example). In the latter scenario this technique is an excellent way of capturing action without manic behaviour from the pupils. It can be 'unfrozen' by moving the action forward in slow motion.

As your work with this technique develops, you might try crafting a storyboard from a series of still images, highlighting the key moments in a text through a series of tableaux. Each can be accompanied by a headline or an extract from the text (particularly valuable when working with Shakespeare). Pupils can even be asked to identify which extracts underpin each tableau and to explain why they chose to represent the section of text in the way they did. This involves pupils in analytical and creative thought about the text they are working with. Volunteers might even be 'sculpted' into still images. In this way, all group members have an input into the posing of the moment and can fruitfully discuss the rationale behind their choices. It is also very powerful to get pupils to hold their tableau for enough time to allow other pupils to explore its three-dimensional qualities and view it from different perspectives.

With a confident, capable group you can work up the tableaux into a modern format such as a film trailer and the narrative can be secured by adding a 'voiceover' which connects up the still images. This is a really interesting adjunct to the exploration of persuasive techniques in other areas of the English curriculum. Thought-tapping also offers capacity to enrich and extend this activity. As teacher you simply tap one of the pupils in the still image on the shoulder and that becomes their cue for them in character to speak their thoughts at that moment.

EMPTY SEAT/HOTSEATING

The term 'hotseating' refers to a drama technique in which a fictional character is questioned by the group of pupils. Normally the pupil (in role) literally sits in the hotseat. As teacher, you can adapt this basic structure imaginatively to suit the specifics of your teaching group. Clearly, a confident pupil can manage the role unaided but, equally, two pupils can represent the character at the same time. Indeed, even you can step into the role. The 'empty seat' is a similar concept but takes the pressure off more nervous or apprehensive pupils. Place a seat at the front of the room with an imaginary character sitting in it. Anyone in the class can ask a question; pupils volunteer to answer as the chosen character. This activity may be used in an improvisatory way, but often it produces better results where both those playing 'characters' and those asking questions have had time to prepare at least something in advance.

CHORAL SPEAKING

There are many kinds of choral speaking activity. The aim is to enable every member of a group to contribute to the presentation of a speech or a series of lines. At a basic level you might simply divide up a speech into a sequence of sense units (see above) which you distribute to individual pupils. You could then ask them to learn their words by speaking them aloud as they walk round the room, using them as a greeting to each other and so on until they are confident in using them. They rebuild the speech by delivering their portion of text in turn. This creates an interesting interplay of different rhythms and voices. Some lines can be spoken in unison by two or more voices, some echoed or repeated. To demonstrate the cumulative energy or dynamic of a speech you might ask the pupils to gradually increase the volume as the speech develops. Pupils can add movement, gesture, sound effects or even music to increase the impact. With more confident pupils working in small groups you might give them a whole poem or speech to perform as a choral reading, exploring techniques such as repetition, relocating portions of text and the use of multiple voice combinations to achieve a variety of effects.

Creative assessment: developing thoughts

- Although there are a number of plays that regularly feature as 'set texts' within English exam specifications (for example, at GCSE: *An Inspector Calls*) there are numerous opportunities to explore prose and poetry through dramatic method. Look back through one of your Schemes of Work and identify how any of the activities outlined in this chapter could be integrated into the Programme of Study.
- Reflect on how and where you could use any of these drama strategies to enhance pupils' responses to other strands of the English curriculum, for example, to generate written work or to enhance reading.
- Consider the issues posed by the need to 'record evidence' of pupils' work in English. How does this impact on the way in which you might view drama? Devise some ideas for collecting information about, and tracking, pupils' achievements and progress. Would you use some kind of written proforma or record sheet as in S&L assessment? Is it better to film or digitally record pupils' work? Is there a place for a more convenient or 'shorthand' method like the use of 'Post-it' notes? Or would you argue the case for not recording pupils' work at all?

CONCLUSIONS

One of the aims of this chapter was to refresh your thinking about the possibilities of dramatic method and how drama strategies can be used to enhance the quality of learning in the classroom. Deliberately, the ideas have been selected because they are practical and achievable within an ordinary classroom environment and because they can be employed without the need for specialist drama training and expertise. Furthermore, there is a belief that as capable and imaginative English teachers who know your own school contexts really well, you will be able to adapt and adjust any of these routines to fit your own specific requirements. All of them offer that degree of flexibility. Each of the ideas has been widely and successfully used in classrooms to develop pupils' social skills, to empower their independent and creative thinking and to further their enjoyment and appreciation of the full range of the English curriculum. The hope is that after working through this chapter you'll be sufficiently intrigued and engaged to try out some of the ideas. They could make a real difference to what happens in your classroom.

RECOMMENDED READING

Berry, C. (1988) *The Actor and his Text*. London: Scribner.

Cox, B. (1989) *English in the National Curriculum*. London: HMSO.

DCSF/QCA (Department for Children, Schools and Families/Qualifications and Curriculum Authority) (2007) The National Curriculum: statutory requirements for key stages 3 and 4. London: DCSF/QCA.

DfE (Department for Education) (2010) *The National Strategies Secondary – Developing Drama in English: A handbook for English subject leaders and teachers*. London: DfE.

DfEE (Department for Education and Employment) (2001) *Key Stage Three National Strategy Framework for Teaching English: Years 7, 8 and 9*. Suffolk: DfEE.

Farmer, D. (2007) *101 Drama Games and Activities*, http://www.lulu.com

Neelands, J. (2012) *Beginning Drama 11–14*. Third edition. London: Routledge.

Stredder, J. (2009) *The North Face of Shakespeare*. Cambridge: Cambridge University Press.

Chapter 6   Media in English

ANDREW GREEN

In this chapter you will consider:

- how the study of media relates to the study of English;
- purposes for the study of media;
- media and literacy;
- a range of practical approaches to using and teaching media.

INTRODUCTION

Long gone are the days when what we understand by 'the media' could be confined to newspapers, magazines, television and film. The range of new media and the almost continual hybridisation of forms pose a constant challenge to teachers of English. Pupils are increasingly fluent users, readers and producers of media text, and the teaching of English needs constantly to develop to reflect these changes. Along with these changes comes the need for teachers regularly to reflect upon the nature of their subject and the fundamental concepts that underpin it. What, for example, do English teachers need to know about techniques of television production? How do we theorise knowledge of multimodal texts? Is literacy a fixed concept? How do we balance technical knowledge with content knowledge when approaching the production of media texts? When dealing with the media we are on constantly shifting ground.

MEDIA STUDIES AND ENGLISH

In beginning our consideration of the teaching of media, it is important to think about how the study of media and the study of English relate to one another and how this relationship is represented in the NC.

Activity 6.1

Thinking about media

- Look closely at the NC. Where does media fit in?
- What is the difference between Media Studies in English and Media Studies as a subject in its own right?

Activity 6.1 *continued*

- Should there be a difference?
- Why does Media Studies exist as a separate subject?
- How does the study of media relate to literary study?
- How does it relate to processes of reading and writing?
- What particular demands does the study of media place on the use of ICT?

It is helpful to start by thinking about what you wish to achieve as a teacher of English through your teaching of media. Jenny Grahame (1990) suggests the following as a set of desirable outcomes. Media education should enable pupils to:

- understand the similarities and differences between the many media around us;
- reflect on their own experience of the media;
- develop a critical language to describe, categorise and analyse the media;
- express themselves in the widest range of media possible.

It is clear from this that the study of media is related to language in very similar ways as is the study of literature. In fact, the word 'literature' could be substituted into Grahame's definition without any difficulty at all. Support for this view becomes clearer if we look at a range of ways in which we might approach media texts (see Figure 6.1). The final column has been left blank for you to write down your thoughts about what you might cover in relation to each of these issues.

What type of text is it?	Categories/genres	
How is it produced?	Technologies	
How do we know what it means?	Languages	
Who is communicating and why?	Agencies	
How does it present its subject?	Representations	
Who receives it and what sense do they make of it?	Audiences	

Figure 6.1 Aspects of media education (adapted from DES/BFI, 1989)

The similarity to paradigms of literary study is again evident. Contrary to the received wisdom that Media Studies and related qualifications are 'easy options', it is clear from this model that the study of media is actually highly theorised. Genre study, the linguistic and structural issues underpinning text, purposes and methods of textual construction, conventions of artistic representation, modes of textual reception and meaning-making are all implied. These are precisely the issues teachers of English tend to address when approaching a wide range of literary and non-literary text.

PURPOSES OF STUDYING MEDIA

The teaching of media, then, emerges naturally from and feeds directly into a holistic vision of English studies, and it is important that as a teacher of English you seek to capitalise upon this by building firm bridges between media and English studies. The UNESCO

Declaration on Media Education made this clear thirty years ago. Although a lengthy statement, this is worth reproducing in full.

GRUNWALD DECLARATION ON MEDIA EDUCATION

We live in a world where media are omnipresent: an increasing number of people spend a great deal of time watching television, reading newspapers and magazines, playing records and listening to the radio. In some countries, for example, children already spend more time watching television than they do attending school.

Rather than condemn or endorse the undoubted power of the media, we need to accept their significant impact and penetration throughout the world as an established fact, and also appreciate their importance as an element of culture in today's world. The role of communication and media in the process of development should not be underestimated, nor the function of media as instruments for the citizen's active participation in society. Political and educational systems need to recognise their obligations to promote in their citizens a critical understanding of the phenomena of communication.

Regrettably most informal and non-formal educational systems do little to promote media education or education for communication. Too often the gap between the educational experience they offer and the real world in which people live is disturbingly wide. But if the arguments for media education as a ~~preparation~~ for responsible citizenship are formidable now, in the very near ~~development~~ of communication technology such as satellite ~~systems~~, television data systems, video cassette and ~~...~~, given the increasing degree of choice ~~...~~ these developments.

~~...~~ these developments, but will work ~~...~~ them and making sense of such consequences ~~...~~ two-way communication and the ensuing ~~...~~tion.

~~...~~ct on cultural identity of the flow of information ~~...~~ the mass media.

~~...~~the responsibility of preparing the young ~~...~~ul images, words and sounds. Children and ~~...~~e of these symbolic systems, and this will ~~...~~tional priorities. Such a reassessment might ~~...~~proach to the teaching of language and

~~...~~ective when parents, teachers, media personnel ~~...~~edge they have a role to play in developing ~~...~~isteners, viewers and readers. The greater inte- ~~...~~munications systems would undoubtedly be an ~~...~~ective education.

~~...~~*npetent authorities to:*

~~...~~prehensive media education programs – from pre- ~~...~~ and in adult education – the purpose of which is to ~~...~~skills and attitudes which will encourage the growth ~~...~~nd, consequently, of greater competence among ~~...~~ and print media. Ideally, such programs should ~~...~~nedia products, the use of media as means of creative

expression, and effective use of and participation in available media channels;

2   develop training courses for teachers and intermediaries both to increase their knowledge and understanding of the media and train them in appropriate teaching methods, which would take into account the already considerable but fragmented acquaintance with media already possessed by many students;

3   stimulate research and development activities for the benefit of media education, from such domains as psychology, sociology, and communication science;

4   support and strengthen the actions undertaken or envisaged by UNESCO and which aim at encouraging international co-operation in media education.

Grunwald, Federal Republic of Germany, 22 January 1982

This statement touches closely upon the purposes for teaching media and the range of issues it encompasses:

- social;
- cultural;
- political;
- educational;
- communication;
- new 'literacies'.

All of these issues naturally have significant implications for the English classroom and it is important that you think personally about them.

Activity 6.2

Personal response

The Grunwald Statement was written thirty years ago. In what ways would you develop this statement to reflect the contemporary state of media education and your personal views of media teaching? Think about what you would add, what you would take away and what you would want to develop to make this a statement of personal philosophy.

What is important above all is to ensure that pupils, who live in an increasingly media-saturated environment, are equipped with the abilities to be effective critical 'readers' and producers in a wide range of media contexts. This is, of course, very difficult when the role of the 'reader' or audience is changing so rapidly and where new technologies mean that the boundaries between consumers and producers are increasingly difficult to define. Media texts are now rarely read in isolation. Instead they are part of a complex interaction of platforms and formats which are closely entwined with politics of media ownership.

The implications of emerging technologies such as Web 2.0 and beyond require teachers to move away from traditional text-based study of media and towards a new exploration of how audiences access, make sense of and interact with texts, and the range of contexts in which they do so. This evidently necessitates a reconsideration of traditional notions of literacy and teachers need to think carefully about how they can and should use these issues in addressing the requirements of the NC.

MEDIA AND LITERACY

It is important to realise that pupils often arrive in school with highly developed media literacy. Very young children, through watching cartoons, come with strongly developed symbolic awareness, understanding about how simple narrative conventions function and how characters can be 'read' according to their clothes, tone of voice and so on. Slightly older pupils will already be used to handling narrative over the length of a feature film and will be able to understand how music is used to manipulate their responses, or will be used to reading comics and magazines aimed at their age group; there are even children's newspapers, like *First News*. They are used, in other words, to responding to a range of media texts and have an innate sense of how such texts are composed (written) and 'read'. By the time pupils arrive in secondary school they are familiar receivers and users of a plurality of media. The challenge for you as their teacher, therefore, is to help your pupils to deconstruct their implicit understanding of how such texts function so that they can become even more effective readers and producers of media.

Evidently, in order to do this, we need to reconsider what we mean by 'reading' and 'writing' in the context of the media. In some forms (e.g. print journalism) this is very close to other forms of written text. But for other forms of media the connection is not so straightforward and we need to work towards a more inclusive definition of literacy and the significance of all forms of text. Film or TV, for example, although we consume them largely (though not exclusively) as seen texts, are often initially developed in written form. And web texts, whilst they may be predominantly in the written medium, require us to read and access text in a variety of ways, not simply in the linear reading mode we usually apply to written text (e.g. we may follow hyperlinks to sites external to the original text in the middle of reading, or readers may follow a range of paths to gain access to material).

Activity 6.3

Media literacy

Consider the following media forms. What types of 'reading' and 'writing' are required for each?

- music video;
- film;
- online advertisement;
- a large multimedia website (e.g. the BBC);
- narrative-based video games;
- magazine;
- mobile phones.

Some major principles to think about are covered below. It is important to recognise that these principles are partially shared, but not synonymous, with those underpinning English study.

Literacy encompasses all communicative texts

Whether in print, words, still or moving images, sound, or online form, in analogue or digital form, and in whatever genre, texts require literate producers and readers. This inclusiveness is central to media education. This raises questions of cultural value, as media teaching at GCSE and A Level eschews prescribed texts or the notion of a textual canon of individual great works. This sets it apart from English and opens it up to the annual barrage of criticism referred to earlier.

Texts are polysemic

Different audiences will bring distinct meanings to and will extract different meanings from texts. This plurality of 'readings' is to be celebrated, as reading is an active and social process. How do your own life experiences and experiences as a learner encourage you (perhaps tacitly) to privilege certain types of text and/or certain approaches to 'reading' and 'writing'? How does this fit into the triangular relationship between the text, its audience and its producer?

All texts are constructs

Whatever their form, genre, mode or platform, all texts are representational constructs. No text is ever value-free. Media studies looks beyond the text and explores the technical means by which views are constructed and the social and cultural factors that influence them. This includes the economic and industrial forces at play.

Pupils must read and write a wide range of texts

To understand text types fully, pupils need to engage with them both as readers and as writers. Whilst many pupils will 'read' and analyse media texts, far fewer are provided with much opportunity to create media texts of their own. Yet, in order to understand how meaning is created through the combination of words, images and sounds in multimodal texts, pupils need such experiences. The NC Programme of Study for writing currently endorses but does not require pupils to produce media texts. In what ways do you feel this limits their ability to engage with media? Would you wish your own pupils to do so? What challenges in terms of subject and technological knowledge does this pose for you?

PRACTICAL APPROACHES TO USING AND TEACHING MEDIA

The possibilities for both using and studying media within the English classroom are enormous. A short selection of ideas follows.

Television/film adaptations

Experiment with using adaptations for both TV and the big screen at various points in the teaching of literary texts: before reading, after reading or alongside reading. What are the pedagogic gains and losses of using adapted versions at each of these stages? What are your personal views on using such adaptations? What advantages do they bring to studying a text? What do they take away? How are they likely to impact on pupil learning? How are they likely to affect pupils' engagement with both texts?

Production and reception

Develop production activities through which pupils can engage with the function of the media industry. This could work, for example, in relation to the teaching of a literary text, but would also serve to integrate detailed issues relating to the study of media. You might wish to address, through this activity, the function of the literary heritage for the media, publishing, broadcasting and other cultural industries, the impact of new media technologies on audiences' reception and interpretation of the literary heritage. Aims for this might be:

- to develop close reading skills around an extract from a set literary text;
- its meanings and interpretation over time and across media;
- the impact on the original text of adaptation from print to moving image; and
- the reasons for its relevance and cultural significance over time.

Commissioning an adaptation

Pupils are tasked with researching for a TV production company the commissioning of a new adaptation. Newspaper articles and reviews of recent adaptations can be used as a starter and they can undertake some limited audience research into the appeal of the project. Consider why canonical literature is so frequently adapted and the ways in which it is approached.

Producing an adaptation

Pupils produce a new adaptation of the text. Develop sample storyboards and scripts for a key scene following a close reading of the original text. Prepare proposals for camerawork, soundtrack, mise-en-scène, editing, appropriate casting and performance. Present these to the class and explain choices and interpretations. Go on to compare the groups' outcomes. To engineer some diversity, you could stipulate certain requirements for different groups (one a classic costume drama, another a contemporary updating, etc.). If possible or desired, pupils can go on to produce their adaptation digitally.

Adaptations over time

Watch extracts from a range of screen adaptations of a single text (silent movies to contemporary). Consider how media 'language' and convention has developed over time. How does this affect the way we view the text? How does the relationship between the original text and the adapted text change between adaptations? What does this tell us about the social and cultural context of the adaptation and its meanings?

Transforming difficult texts

Try using media technology to provide pupils with a way into difficult texts (e.g. Shakespeare). Pour an extract of text into a word-cloud or similar software application, collapse it and identify key adjectives and recurrent nouns. Now devise a fictitious product, working with the language to create an advertisement based on the original text extract. This enables pupils creatively to explore the nature of language and the symbolic nature of text in both literary and media form.

Using images

Pupils are introduced to a text, a picture, a musical stimulus, a location, a concept, etc. They are then tasked with producing an image response to this. You may wish to provide a range of images – as hard copies, or in digital form – or pupils may be given a totally free choice. They may even wish to create their own images which must relate literally or symbolically to the original stimulus. They feed back to the teacher or class the reasons for their choices of image. PowerPoint, or software such as Photo Story or iPhoto may be used. Compare pupils' differing image banks, and use these as a springboard to explore differing interpretations and intentions. How does the new 'image'-text relate to the original stimulus and how does the interaction of the stimulus and the new text open up new avenues of meaning?

'Images' into writing

Pupils can create their own digital image-bank, or construct and edit a moving image text. A soundtrack can be included as well if you wish. Discuss with the pupils why they chose to sequence the images in the order they did. What are the effects of juxtaposing particular images? What symbolic and narrative possibilities do these combinations suggest? If a soundtrack has been used, what new dimensions does this add? Is the music congruous or incongruous? What dimensions does this add to the symbolic and narrative 'meanings'? These can then be used as a personally developed stimulus to writing.

TV talk

Provide pupils with a short transcript of TV talk. They must annotate the transcript with comments on language features, tone and register. Perhaps provide different groups with different transcripts. Next, listen to the TV extracts to which the transcripts relate. Evaluate the impact of voice, register, dialect, additional sound, and timing. Finally watch the full extract. Consider how body language, mise-en-scène, framing and camera shots, insert and cutaway extracts, and visual edits add to meaning. This allows sophisticated analysis of layers of meaning-making in the show and engages with how spoken language varies according to the range, demographic and functions of the speakers, and how it is mediated by the format of the show and its editing processes.

Writing and media

Provide opportunities for your pupils to create, not simply to respond to media texts. You do not need advanced technology to do this. Storyboarding, developing treatments, screenplays, or sequences of 'found' images can all be used to prompt pupils into thinking about how differing media texts are structured and function. Storyboards, for example, can be used to explore the role of visual story-telling and characterisation. Mobile technologies, like digital cameras, flip cameras, video cameras, iPads and mobile phones can also be used to great effect as capture devices. The technology is easily used and can provide instant possibilities for sharing the outcomes of written work with the whole class. Using software such as PicturePower 3 or Photo Story, pupils can easily sequence, crop and edit images, developing voice-over commentaries on a vast range of topics, and these can, if desired, feed into more formal written work.

Adapting literary texts

Film and television adaptations of literary works abound. Why not try working with your classes on their own adaptations of a text they are studying. This process can provide fascinating insights into how both the original text and the screen medium function. If you have the equipment, the time and the courage, you could even have the pupils shoot and edit their own short adaptations. Figures 6.2, 6.3 and 6.4 below are three short examples of a screen adaptation of *Pride and Prejudice* by Fay Weldon, each annotated to indicate the issues teachers may wish to explore when thinking about transforming literary texts for the screen.

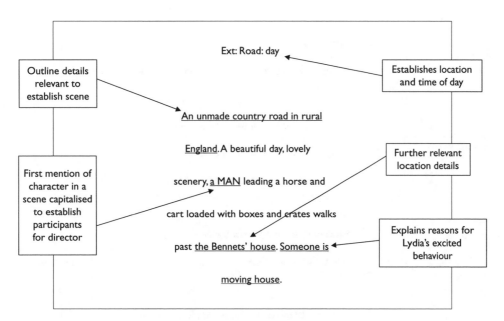

Figure 6.2 Screen adaptation of *Pride and Prejudice* by Fay Weldon – Example 1

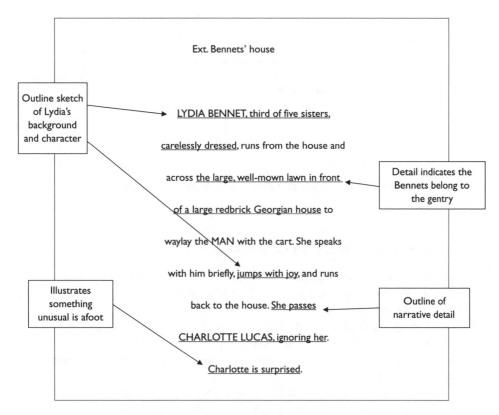

Figure 6.3 Screen adaptation of *Pride and Prejudice* by Fay Weldon – Example 2

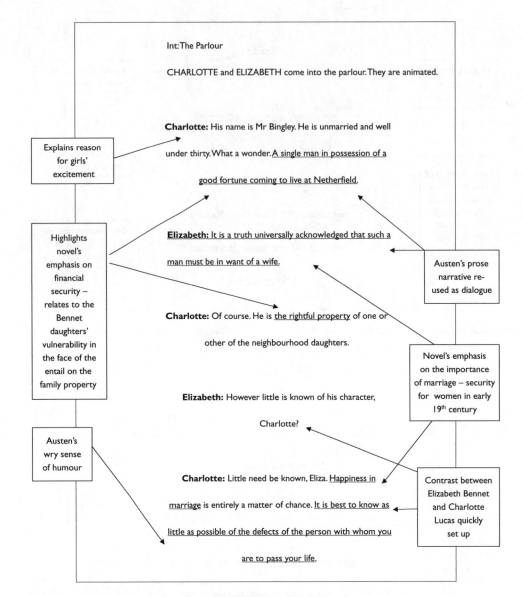

Figure 6.4 Screen adaptation of *Pride and Prejudice* by Fay Weldon – Example 3

Creative assessment: Working with media

- develop narrative re-tellings in a range if different media of source texts;
- devise alternative soundtracks for films to amplify or change their meanings;
- construct directors' commentaries;
- recreate narratives in entirely different formats – e.g. novel as news report; Big Brother as a poem and explore the transformational effects;
- re-edit film or TV texts to create alternative narratives, explaining the rationale and impact of the changes;
- use DVD or CD covers to explore the concept of 'image'; how are visual images, text, font, layout, lyrics, blurbs, critic comments and so on used to create our impression of a particular band, film or product?
- use narrative-based role-play games (e.g. Batman or Runescape) to explore notions of characterisation and narrative and look at how the players of these games become co-constructors of narrative.

CONCLUSIONS

Media has an exciting and essential role to play in the English classroom. It is important not to allow your view of the subject to be tainted by the annual round of criticism that faces GCSE and A Level media qualifications. As this chapter has made clear, the study of media as a representation of language is a complex and theoretical activity. Pupils need to be taught how to read and produce in a wide variety of media genres, as these are increasingly the stuff of everyday communication. Critical engagement with the means of media production and the methods media texts employ to create meaning has forced a fundamental change in how language and text are conceived, and the work that you as a teacher undertake in the English classroom needs to shift to take this into account.

RECOMMENDED READING

British Film Institute (2000) *Moving Images in the Classroom*. London: BFI.

Burn, A. (n.d.) *Media*. Available at http://www.ite.org.uk/ite_topics/media/001.html (accessed on 7 March 2011).

Burn, A. and Durran, J. (2007) *Media Literacy in Schools: Practice, Production and Progression*. London: Paul Chapman.

Burn, A. and Durrant, C. (2008) *Media Teaching*. Sheffield: NATE.

DES/BFI (Department of Education and Science/British Film Institute) (1989) *Primary Media Education: A Curriculum Statement*. London: British Film Institute.

Fleming, M. and Stevens, D. (2004) Media Education, in M. Fleming and D. Stevens, *English Teaching in the Secondary School*. London: David Fulton, pp. 167–78.

Grahame, J. (1990) *The English Curriculum: Media*. London: English and Media Centre.

Grahame, J. and Green, A. (2011) Media in English, in A. Green (ed.) *Becoming a Reflective English Teacher*. Maidenhead: McGraw-Hill, pp. 140–55.

Scarratt, E. and McInnes, R. (2009) Media Education and ICT, in J. Davison and J. Dowson (eds) *Learning to Teach English in the Secondary School*. London: Routledge, pp. 178–217.

Chapter 7   Teaching language

ISHMAEL LEWIS

In this chapter you will consider:

- the place of language teaching in the NC;
- teaching language in the English classroom;
- some of the context and perspectives attached to language teaching;
- approaches and tasks for language skills teaching;
- how to engage pupils in developing their own language skills for a variety of purposes.

INTRODUCTION

Most of you reading this will have a certificate or two which provide some evidence of your competence in English language. The teaching and learning of English language is the key focus of the NC Orders for English (QCA, 2007; DCELLS, 2008) and will form the basis of much of your teaching. At degree level, however, the study of English seems to be more usually the study of literature. For many of you, your most recent studies will have involved analysing and exploring literary texts rather than aspects of language. It is also fairly probable that many of you would fairly quickly identify English Literature as the study of prose, poetry and drama and see attainment as being linked closely to the depth and detail of your understanding and analysis. English language, however, seems to be both broader and more difficult to pin down.

As a teacher of English, it is important that you consider what English language means in your classroom and how you can approach a subject that is wide ranging and seems to appeal to a variety of views of the purpose of language teaching. Many beginning teachers feel some tension between the teaching of accuracy and providing opportunities for pupils to explore their own language in their own way. The focus of this chapter will be to consider some of the ways in which aspects of language teaching can be approached in the classroom, whilst also giving some consideration to its role and purpose.

CONTEXT

The place, purpose and expectations of language teaching in the NC is something of a hot potato and has been subject to several debates and revisions since its introduction. Indeed, since the emergence of English as a discrete subject for study in the late 1800s, notions of purpose have been central to the ways in which the subject has been configured. In 1921 the Newbolt Report (Wyse and Jones, 2007) saw the teaching of Standard English as a central element in the creation of a more equal and mobile society. This call for the teaching of Standard English has been repeated by many. Others, however, have claimed that diversity and difference are important aspects of language development. Bullock (1975) in his influential report noted that pupils' language may take a variety of forms and that this diversity was to be explored and valued rather than eradicated. Bullock moved the focus onto 'appropriateness' rather than 'correctness'.

The influence of this important distinction can still be seen today (see Cowley (2003) for a more thorough exploration of this). Cox (1989) also recognised that language is dynamic and that, whilst the teaching of a standard form of English had clear merit, this merit was linked to particular places and purposes. He also recognised that dialect and other language forms have merit and should not be brushed aside. These debates seem to stem from different models of teaching and learning and seem to prioritise different functions of language. Cox (1989) identified five models of English teaching. They are not mutually exclusive, nor even sharply distinguishable and all are important aspects of your responsibility as an English teacher.

Activity 7.1

Aspects of language

Look at Figure 7.1, which outlines Cox's models for English, and consider how each model may be evidenced or inform aspects of your teaching of language.

Cox's model	In the classroom
1. Personal growth – *focuses on the child: it emphasises the relationship between language and learning in the individual child, and the role of literature in developing children's imaginative and aesthetic lives.*	
2. Cultural heritage – *emphasises the responsibility of schools to lead children to an appreciation of those works of literature that have been widely regarded as the finest in our language.*	
3. Cultural analysis – *emphasises the role of English in helping children towards a critical understanding of the world and cultural environment in which they live. Children should know about the processes by which meanings are conveyed, and about the ways in which print and other media carry values.*	
4. Adult needs – *focuses on communication outside the school: it emphasises the responsibility of English teachers to prepare children for the language demands of adult life, including the workplace, in a fast-changing world.*	
5. Cross-curricular – *focuses on the school: it emphasises that all teachers have a responsibility to help children with the language demands of different subjects on the school curriculum.*	

Figure 7.1 Cox's models

ENGLISH LANGUAGE AND THE NC

As a new entrant into the teaching profession, it is important that you identify your own ethos and priorities as a secondary English teacher. Also, irrespective of your individual priorities as a teacher of English, it should be remembered that the NC is, for most of you, a statutory document and your expectations must be worked into what is a very crowded curriculum. The NC states that English is

> vital for communicating with others in school and in the wider world, and is fundamental to learning in all curriculum subjects. In studying English, pupils develop skills in speaking, listening, reading and writing that they will need to participate in society and employment. Pupils learn to express themselves creatively and imaginatively and to communicate with others confidently and effectively.
>
> (QCA, 2007)

Here the functional and expressive, personal and societal aspects of English language teaching can be seen. Figure 7.2 outlines the key concepts (the '4 Cs' as they are known) which underpin the language elements of the NC (QCA, 2007). To the right-hand side is space for you to consider which (if any) of Cox's models seems to fit with each of these concepts, and also to consider tasks and activities you could employ that would support and develop learning in each area.

As can be seen, the key concepts which underpin the NC seem to draw together fairly disparate elements from all sides of the debate around the teaching of language. These key concepts give some idea of the scope and variety of language teaching in the English classroom. Given the broad range of aspects, skills and concepts that make up the language part of English as a curriculum subject, these concepts endeavour to consolidate a number of views regarding what 'English' should mean in the classroom. They cover many of the facets of the subject of English language as discussed above and, as such, will be used as an organising framework for the following sections. The main focus will be on *competence* and *creativity*, although all four concepts will be discussed.

Competence Being clear, coherent and accurate in spoken and written communication. Demonstrating a secure understanding of the conventions of written language, including grammar, spelling and punctuation. Being adaptable in a widening range of familiar and unfamiliar contexts within the classroom and beyond. Making informed choices about effective ways to communicate formally and informally.	Cox's model: Sample tasks and activities
Creativity Making fresh connections between ideas, experiences, texts and words, drawing on a rich experience of language and literature. Using inventive approaches to making meaning, taking risks, playing with language and using it to create new effects. Using imagination to convey themes, ideas and arguments, solve problems, and create settings, moods and characters. Using creative approaches to answering questions, solving problems and developing ideas.	Cox's model: Sample tasks and activities
Cultural understanding Understanding how English varies locally and globally, and how these variations relate to identity and cultural diversity.	Cox's model: Sample tasks and activities
Critical understanding Assessing the validity and significance of information and ideas from different sources. Exploring others' ideas and developing their own. Analysing and evaluating spoken and written language to appreciate how meaning is shaped.	Cox's model: Sample tasks and activities

Figure 7.2 Curriculum concepts

COMPETENCE

Concept definition

In terms of the teaching of language, how would *you* define 'competence'? Use no more than ten words.
What most interests you about this aspect?
Where do you think you may have to consolidate your own understanding?

The notion of competence includes, but is not reducible to, more functional aspects of language teaching such as grammar, punctuation, spelling. Accuracy, the ability to recognise when and how to use Standard English, and clarity and coherence are all important aspects of this part of language teaching.

As a starting point, consult the NC Orders that apply to you and identify which elements pertain to the teaching and learning of spelling, grammar and punctuation. Figure 7.3 identifies some examples from the Orders for Wales and England. Consider also, any aspects that you think are more broadly concerned with competence.

You may well have found it relatively straightforward to identify which elements of the curriculum should go into the right-hand column. In the Orders for England, for example, the technical accuracy section for writing is pretty much wholly concerned with grammar, punctuation and spelling. You may, however, have found yourself debating whether certain elements belonged in the left-hand column. Would enabling pupils to 'understand how meaning is created through the combination of words, images and sounds in multimodal texts' belong in the left-hand column in this 'Competence' skill area (QCA, 2007: 65)? Would it perhaps belong in 'Creativity'? Or might it fit best in 'Critical Understanding'? The concepts, much like Cox's models and language skills themselves, are not discrete, but rather interact with and inform one another.

Your pupils will come to you with differing levels of competence, awareness and experience of using language. Some of your pupils may not have access to Standard English in written or oral form. How you best meet the needs of your pupils is, again, open to debate. Broadly, there are two key approaches. The first approach (see Hudson (2001) for a concise discussion of this), stresses the importance of the systematic teaching of grammar, punctuation and spelling in discrete lessons. Often these lessons are dedicated to one aspect or rule of grammar at a time, building up to broader coverage. Others think that language skills are not learned in that way. Rather, a more contextualised approach is recommended, where pupils learn about language through experience and immersion in a language-rich environment. In this view, pupils' knowledge about and skills in language develop over time, at different rates and through using language themselves.

This has some links to Vygotsky's ideas about the importance of language being internalised. It is important to remember that teaching something is not the same as that thing being learned. As a teacher, you must consider the needs of your pupils and what sorts of approaches would provide them with the best opportunity to develop their skills. Remember that the teaching of grammar and punctuation is not an end in itself. It is there to support and extend pupils' reading, writing and S&L. Pupils may well be able to

Grammar, punctuation and spelling	Other elements of competence
Use a range of sentence structures, linking them coherently and developing the ability to use paragraphs effectively (DCELLS, 2008). Use grammar accurately in a variety of sentence types, including subject–verb agreement and correct and consistent use of tense (QCA, 2007).	Structure their writing to support the purpose of the task and guide the reader (QCA, 2007).

Figure 7.3 Competence in language

complete exercises on the correct use of the apostrophe successfully, but this does not necessarily mean that this awareness will be sustained nor that it will impact upon their writing when they are writing independently.

You will need to make a decision as to whether you wish to teach certain aspects of competent language use as discrete activities or lessons, or whether you are going to use a more embedded approach. It is important that you understand *why* you have chosen a particular approach for a particular set of learners.

Activity 7.2

Planning and rationale

Figure 7.4 may be useful for planning. I have provided examples (not necessarily reflective of my own views). You could (and should), of course, identify where and why you could use both discrete and embedded approaches to teach and reinforce an aspect of grammar, punctuation and so on.

Element	Discrete	Embedded	Rationale
Apostrophe use.	Whole lesson focusing in on the possessive apostrophe.		Most of class 8F do not use apostrophes for possession in their written work. A discrete focus is needed to embed the rules for apostrophe use.

Figure 7.4 Planning and rationale

You may decide that having discrete, rule focussed lessons is not enough – pupils need to see and experience language in use for it to make real sense. You may also decide that immersion is also, in itself, not enough – pupils need to understand rules for certain aspects of grammar, as they will not simply pick them up through language experiences. You may decide that both approaches have merit and can be used to reinforce one another. What is most important is that your pupils are given the opportunity to develop competence (and then confidence) as language users – in whatever way or ways you judge to be most effective for them.

CREATIVITY

Concept definition

In terms of the teaching of language, how would *you* define 'creativity'? Use no more than ten words.
What most interests you about this aspect?
Where do you think you may have to consolidate your own understanding?

Creativity is sometimes neglected in secondary schools. Creative writing, for instance, is sometimes taught through a collection of desired or required effects and devices as if these elements were all there is to creating an exciting or engaging piece of writing. If you are really to encourage pupils to make 'fresh connections' and 'use imagination' (QCA, 2007), then this approach may, on its own, be a little reductive.

As aspects of reading, writing and oracy are broken down into teachable parts, important creative elements are sometimes forgotten. Tasks and approaches that encourage pupils to use and develop their imaginations are an essential part of your classroom practice. However, often pupils' creative writing is rather formulaic: one mention of each sense (sometimes a little stretched when it comes to smell and taste), two metaphors, a simile and an example of onomatopoeia. Whilst these elements can, and often do, provide creative 'hooks' for pupils' language use, they are less to do with creativity and more to do with some formulaic notion of competence. Importantly, encouraging our pupils to be creative users of language is not just about 'creative writing'. The key aspects of this element of the curriculum are:

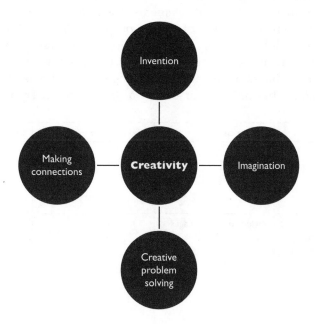

Figure 7.5 Creativity

This can present a rather tricky classroom dilemma; how do you teach pupils to be inventive, independent problem solvers able to make fresh connections of their own? Some elements of this will be looked at in the section on Critical Understanding. What is necessary here, however, is that, as teachers, we broaden our understanding of what creativity means in our classrooms.

Creative assessment: Creativity

Consider the four key elements of Creativity in Figure 7.5 and look at where they match the skills, content and range elements of the NC Programme of Study.

- Did you find many explicit references to the four key aspects of creativity?
- Where did you find them?
- Can you see places where these creative aspects of language could be used in other aspects of range and content/skills?
- Are other aspects of language represented more explicitly?

Sometimes, pupils seem out of practice when it comes to independent and creative thinking. Try to give pupils the opportunity to use language to invent, connect and experiment. Figure 7.6 offers some starting points for creative engagement in the classroom. Complete the table as best fits one or more of your classes.

These ideas are just starting points. Many more can be found in, for example, Robert Fisher's *Games for Thinking* (1997). What is important is that pupils are given the opportunity to use and develop language as tools for creative thinking.

You will, of course, also be teaching children about how to use language imaginatively in their writing of narrative. At Figures 7.7 and 7.8 you will find two outline images (Cooze, 2007). These can be used as starting points for creative writing of any kind. The outline of the body is used to encourage pupils to imagine how their body may react in a given situation. In a scary situation, for example, the hairs on the back of their necks may stand up, or their knees may go weak. The outline of the home can be used in a similar way. Pupils can label their diagrams with elements of sympathetic background. To continue the theme, stairs may creak, the eyes of figures on posters may follow you around the room and so on. As well as labelling, pupils should be encouraged to add detail to the diagrams – they can draw in facial features, weather, or parts of the house, its background and its contents. These diagrams can act as a starting point and make for a more creative style of writing frame. They are, of course, only a starting point. Try to think of ways in

Task	Resources	Learning Objective	Creative language skills
Invent an animal Pupils invent a new animal. You may wish to specify the environment in which the animal will live.			
Connect Four Pupils individually or in pairs are given four objects/images/words to connect creatively.	Various objects, images etc.		
What do we have here? Provide pupils with a series of 'clues', some objects and some brief details regarding a crime scene. They have to come up with a plausible explanation for events. You may, if you wish, extend this by adding new details, evidence or twists at key points.			
Concept Stretching Present pupils with a question which will elicit diverse opinions (e.g. 'Are cats the best pets?' or 'Is the death penalty wrong?'). Pupils physically place themselves along a line of agreement – strongly agree at one end, strongly disagree at the other and all points in between. Pupils have to explain and explore the reasons why they have placed themselves and move along the line as they are persuaded otherwise.			

Figure 7.6 Creativity tasks

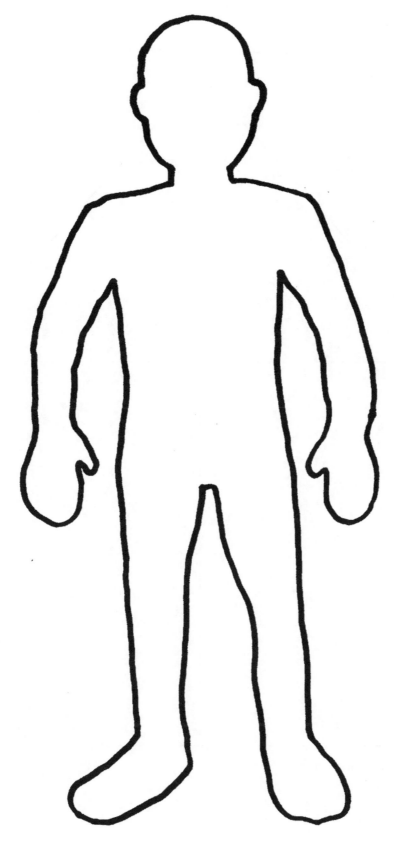

Figure 7.7 Outline image – Body

Figure 7.8 Outline image – Home

which you get pupils to engage with and imagine an event, a situation, a setting and so on that are creative rather than simply formulaic. Return to the NC and look at where and how imaginative skills appear. Consider how, or if, the skill level builds upon that found in the preceding level. This may also help you see what aspects of imaginative language use are explicitly featured and where the features and development are broad and open. It should also encourage you to consider whether imagination can be taught sequentially.

Activity 7.4

Teaching creativity

Consider the fuller statement of the place of creativity in the English classroom:

> *Creativity:* Pupils show creativity when they make unexpected connections, use striking and original phrases or images, approach tasks from a variety of starting points, or change forms to surprise and engage the reader. Creativity can be encouraged by providing purposeful opportunities for pupils to experiment, build on ideas or follow their own interests. Creativity in English extends beyond narrative and poetry to other forms and uses of language. It is essential in allowing pupils to progress to higher levels of understanding and become independent.
>
> (QCA, 2007: 62)

- Is there some inherent difficulty in 'teaching' this sort of creativity?
- Consider places in the level descriptors where this sort of creativity can be evidenced.
- Are you given specific guidance in the Programmes of Study or the Level Descriptors regarding what aspects of imaginative language use should be taught?

CULTURAL UNDERSTANDING

Concept definition: cultural understanding

In terms of the teaching of language, how would *you* define 'cultural understanding'?
Use no more than ten words.
What most interests you about this aspect?
Where do you think you may have to consolidate your own understanding?

'Bad' language is a concept that pupils will be familiar with. Discussions about language can seem essentially concerned with the idea that language use exists in the traditional binary arrangement of 'correct' or 'incorrect'. A far more useful concept, introducing as it does the idea of adapting register to suit purpose, text conventions and audience, is the idea that certain types of expression simply work better in certain contexts than others. This allows language users flexibility in their choices, rather than simply being wrong or right. Broadly, effective communication and expression is all about the individual making a variety of choices, both in terms of content and style. Allied to this should be the idea that different situations require different forms of language choices (at word, sentence or text levels). Some of this can be approached through exploring literature, and it is essential that pupils are given access to a wide repertoire of language to enable them to make effective language choices. In this, language forms other than Standard English have merit and value.

Activity 7.5

Language cultures

The notion of 'culture' can be difficult to pin down. As human beings we frequently exist in a range of cultures (work, home, the Arts, social, etc.), each of which require differing language functions. Your pupils will already use a variety of forms of language for a range of purposes. Some of your pupils may well also use a number of languages for different purposes. Ask pupils to keep a language diary for a day (or longer if you think it would be useful). This can help provide you, and your pupils, with a sense of how wide and diverse their language use is. It may even be helpful to complete one yourself as it can give you a more context-based awareness of the sorts of language forms and codes you use, too. Figure 7.9 may provide a useful structure.

Language diaries like this provide a fascinating basis to consider notions of appropriateness and purpose of language use. You may wish to select one language episode from a pupil's diary and ask them to give it another audience and/or purpose. Ask pupils to consider:

- What changed in terms of the words they chose?
- Did they use different punctuation or grammar?
- Why did they make the changes that they did?

This can be developed further in a number of ways such as giving pupils a piece of text written with a particular audience and purpose in mind. Ask pupils to decide what the audience and purpose may be and also to consider the reasons behind their answer. Pupils can then rewrite or speak the text for a quite different audience and purpose. You can give them all the same audience and purpose or, more interestingly, give a number of quite

Situation/place	Language used to . . .	Language mode	Special words or terms	Questions or comments . . .
On way to school.	Tell my friend I was going to the dentist.	Text.	l8; m8; ABT2.	I didn't write in sentences or use any punctuation. Why can't all words be spelled like that all the time? It's quicker.

Figure 7.9 Language cultures

different ones in order to elicit a greater variety of responses. Pupils can then swap responses and see if they can work out the intended audience and purpose. You could also read out a simple notice or set of instructions written in an unfamiliar dialect form. Ask them to consider how they felt, how they could respond and what may help them understand. Give pupils a particular dialect to research and ask them to translate a short piece of text into that dialect. You could even ask pupils to learn how different parts of the country pronounce words differently, too. Aspects of language use in the UK can be explored though the very well organised British Library website: http://www.bl.uk/learning/langlit/sounds/regional-voices/

Part of cultural understanding is developing an awareness of the global aspects of language use as well as the personal, local and national. It is important that pupils develop an awareness of linguistic diversity. Rather than simply have a display in your classroom about diverse languages, ask pupils to explore and research languages themselves. Give each pupil a language that they have to research. You should decide upon key areas of focus such as:

Language	Where is it spoken? By how many people?	Language family	Writing system	Words for 'hello', 'water', 'food' plus two words of your choice	Interesting fact	Links to our community

Pupils can then transfer this information onto a large world map, drawing in links and identifying key features. This information once gathered can provide a rich starting point for discussion about how languages develop and change, how they are informed and influenced by global shifts (and in turn influence them), and how language may well change in the future.

CRITICAL UNDERSTANDING

Concept definition: critical understanding

In terms of the teaching of language, how would *you* define 'critical understanding'? Use no more than ten words.
What most interests you about this aspect?
Where do you think you may have to consolidate your own understanding?

The fuller statement regarding this important underpinning concept reads as follows:

Critical understanding: Pupils develop critical understanding when they examine uses of language and forms of media and communication, including literary texts, information texts and the spoken word. Developing critical skills allows pupils to challenge ideas, interpretations and assumptions on the grounds of logic, evidence or argument, and is essential if pupils are to form and express their own views independently.

(QCA, 2007: 64)

Consider which aspects of this definition are familiar parts of English lessons you have taught or observed and which seem less familiar to you.

Aspect of critical understanding	Classroom example

It could be argued that a great deal of time is spent in the English classroom encouraging pupils to develop the skills to read and analyse literary texts with focus and purpose. It is also quite usual to find pupils spending time analysing media and information texts, as well as the spoken word. What may not be quite so easy to place within Schemes of Work or experiences are the opportunities to develop the other skills outlined in the definition of critical understanding. These elements seem to be concerned with developing informed and reasoned opinions, evaluating language independently and logically, interpreting and appraising personal opinions and the views of others.

Though not explicitly mentioned in the English Language Programme of Study, thinking skills exercises (e.g. games for thinking, Philosophy for Children inquiry, and aspects of philosophy) help pupils develop crucial skills of problem solving, flexibility and resilience which will develop their independence and competence in English language. If pupils have an awareness of how to follow lines of reasoning, then their ability to use language purposefully and powerfully, as well as to understand the ways in which language is used to construct opinions they have developed a useful set of abilities indeed.

Aspects of A Level Philosophy and/or Critical Thinking (see, for example, AQA or OCR subject websites) work can be used effectively in the English classroom. Consider, for example, the following basic examples of syllogism:

All fish have fins	All dogs have four legs
Goldie is a fish	The chair has four legs
Goldie has fins	The chair is a dog

- Are they both correct?
- Why?
- Which aspect of critical understanding could be developed through using syllogisms?
- How could you use this to develop pupils' critical language skills?
- How could this be adapted for a range of pupils?

There is, of course, a variety of approaches that can be brought into the English classroom from critical thinking or philosophy. It is important, however, that the basic skills are adapted for the needs of the particular class or pupil. All pupils could benefit from developing an awareness of how reasonable (or not) an opinion or conclusion is. Not all pupils, however, would need to know the terms 'syllogism' or 'logical fallacy'. Rather, you could think about adapting the basic principles, using, for example sorting cards, odd one out games, images and so on, so that all pupils are given the opportunity to develop their skills in this area.

A key aspect of critical understanding is active engagement – with ideas, with words and with how they come about. Philosophy for Children is a talk-based thinking skills approach which provides opportunities for pupils to develop their skills of reasoning and criticality through enquiry. The approach is focused on dialogue and has 4 Cs of its own: Caring, Collaboration, Creativity and Criticality. Pupils are given the opportunity to devise questions, develop reasoning and explore ideas as part of a community of enquiry (see Lipman, 2003; Fisher, 2001; and Trickey and Topping, 2004, amongst others for a more detailed discussion). There are a considerable number of organisations – the Society for Advancing Philosophical Enquiry and Reflection in Education (SAPERE), for example – and websites such as http://teachertools.londongt.org/index. php?page=philosophyForChildren that can provide you with some stimulating and engaging ideas for Philosophy for Children based approaches to help develop your pupils' use of language.

Activity 7.6

Critical thinking

Use Figure 7.10 to assess your own awareness and also to consider how these tools could develop pupils' critical language skills. It is not exhaustive and you can add elements and approaches as your own knowledge and experience develops.

Aspect	Own understanding	Language skill development	Classroom approaches/ possible adaptations
Philosophy for Children			
The language of logic (logical fallacies etc)			
Genre			
Constructing and deconstructing argument			
Signposting language			
Semiotics			
Questioning			

Figure 7.10 Critical thinking

CONCLUSIONS

Language teaching in the English classroom is very broad and diverse. The NC of Wales and England seem to recognise this, at least in theory. In practice, you may feel that certain aspects of language are given priority in the curriculum. When considering the spectrum of aspects you need to consider in your teaching of language in the English classroom, you may find it useful to regularly audit your own skills and breadth of knowledge as a teacher of language skills. As teachers, we too have to develop and demonstrate our competence, creativity, cultural understanding and criticality. It is also important to remember that the huge range of and scope of language teaching in the English classroom provides exciting possibilities for pupil and teacher alike.

RECOMMENDED READING

Bullock, A (1975) *A Language for Life: The Bullock Report*. London: HMSO.

Clarke, S., Dickinson, P. and Westbrook, J. (2009) *The Complete Guide to Becoming an English Teacher*. London: Sage.

Cooze, A. (2007) *100+ Ideas for Teaching English*. London: Continuum.

Cowley, T. (2003) *Standard English and the Politics of Language*. London: Macmillan.

Cox, B. (1989) *English in the National Curriculum*. London: HMSO.

DCELLS (The Department for Children, Education, Lifelong Learning and Skills) (2008) *English in the National Curriculum for Wales*. Cardiff: DCELLS.

ESTYN (Her Majesty's Inspectorate for Education and Training in Wales) (2008) *Best practice in the reading and writing of pupils aged 7 to 14 years*. Cardiff: ESTYN.

Fisher, R. (1997) *Games for Thinking*. Oxford: Nash Pollock.

Fisher, R. (2001) 'Philosophy in Primary Schools: fostering thinking skills and literacy', *Reading*, July 2001, pp. 67–73.

Goodwin, P. (2010) *The Literate Classroom*. London: Routledge.

Green, A. (ed.) (2011) *Becoming a Reflective English Teacher*. Maidenhead: Open University Press.

Hudson, D. (2001) Grammar teaching and writing skills, *Syntax in the Schools*, 17: 1–6. Available at http://www.phon.ucl.ac.uk/home/dick/writing.htm

Lipman, M. (2003) *Thinking in Education*. Cambridge: Cambridge University Press.

Murris, K. (1992) *Teaching Philosophy with Picture Books*. London: Infonet Publications.

QCA (Qualifications and Curriculum Authority) (2007) *Programme of study for key stage 3 and attainment targets*. London: QCA.

Trickey, S. and Topping, K. J. (2004) Philosophy for Children: a Systematic Review, *Research Papers in Education*, 19(3): 365–80.

Wyse, D. and Jones, R. (2007) *Teaching English Language and Literacy*. London: Routledge.

Chapter 8   Teaching poetry

ANDREW GREEN

In this chapter you will:

- consider your personal experiences and views of poetry;
- reflect on your poetry subject knowledge;
- consider what you hope to achieve through the teaching of poetry;
- think about the role of poetic terms in teaching poetry;
- explore a number of pedagogic approaches to the teaching of poetry;
- look at how writing poetry can develop pupils' abilities as readers of poetry.

INTRODUCTION

What was your experience of poetry at school? It may be that you loved it. It filled your life with light and inspiration. I hope that is the case. For many pupils (and their teachers), however, the experience of poetry may have been very different. Perhaps for you poetry was not a positive part of your experience of learning English and you dreaded the moment your English teacher would announce, 'Right class, we're going to look at poetry today.' Maybe you think of poetry, and therefore the teaching of poetry, as something difficult.

This need not be the case. Poems are texts and are not difficult simply because they *are* poems. True *some* poems are difficult, but so are *some* novels, *some* plays, *some* works of non-fiction and *some* films. Poetry is simply a different genre and not something automatically hard because it is a poem.

As you start working through this chapter, it is important to reflect on your own experiences of poetry and to use these reflections as a springboard for preparing for your teaching of poetry. It will be helpful for you to spend some time thinking this through. Activity 8.1 will help with this.

Activity 8.1

Your experience of poetry

Take some space and time to reflect on the questions below. This will be useful preparation not only for the work you will do in this chapter, but also for your teaching of poetry in school. Being prepared to challenge your own presuppositions

---

Activity 8.1 *continued*

is one of the hallmarks of an effective teacher, and so it is important to spend time coming to terms with what those presuppositions are.

1   Jot down some thoughts about your own experiences of poetry at school. What was it like? Exciting? Challenging? Incomprehensible? Dull?
2   How did your teachers make you feel about poetry? That it was approachable? That it was distant? That you were free to 'play' with it? That it was to be revered?
3   How did your teachers set about teaching you poetry? Try to remember a range of the pedagogic approaches they adopted.
4   What are you hoping to achieve when you teach poetry?
5   How does this relate to what you are trying to achieve in other areas of the English curriculum?
6   How does it differ?

VIEWS OF POETRY

Philip Larkin writes interestingly on the composition and reception of poetry in 'The Pleasure Principle' (*Required Writings*, 2002), pointing out that poetry can actually be a very simple thing:

> It is sometimes useful to remind ourselves of the simpler aspects of things normally regarded as complicated. Take, for instance, the writing of a poem. It consists of three stages: the first is when a man becomes obsessed with an emotional concept to such a degree that he is compelled to do something about it. What he does is the second stage, namely, construct a verbal device that will reproduce this emotional concept in anyone who cares to read it, anywhere, any time. The third stage is the recurrent situation of people in different times and places setting off the device and re-creating in themselves what the poet felt when he wrote it.

As a teacher of English your job in working with poetry is to help your pupils engage in the act of re-creation that Larkin identifies. As he goes on to observe, this is the most important stage in the life cycle of the poem: '. . . if there is no third stage, no successful reading, the poem can hardly be said to exist at all' (ibid.).

Activity 8.2

Larkin on poetry

Look at what Larkin says here about poetry and think about the following questions:

- Explain your response to Larkin's assertion that these are simple processes.
- How good are you, as a reader, at engaging with the re-creation of a poet's meaning?
- How can you, as a teacher, help pupils to engage in these acts of re-creation?

Maybe you agree with Larkin, and maybe you do not. Perhaps for you the process of (re)creating meaning is pleasurable and simple. It is not hard to understand why pupils (and their teachers) sometimes find the experience of poetry difficult, though. Poems (at least most of the poems pupils will study at school) tend to be short. And when we are dealing with short poems, we often have to do a lot of work with comparatively few words. Besides which, a lot of poetry is hard. Even T. S. Eliot, the master of the hard poem, admitted as much: 'I know that some of the poetry to which I am most devoted is poetry which I did not understand at first reading; some is poetry which I am not sure I understand yet . . .' (T. S. Eliot, 'The Use of Poetry and the Use of Criticism', 1933).

Perhaps part of the problem here is that we all (our pupils included) cling to the familiar. And for pupils of English in schools, the rarefied world of poetry is a radical departure from the world of words and reading that they usually inhabit. As teachers you need to recognise this, but you must be careful not to create difficulties. If you suggest to your pupils that approaching poetry (or indeed any area of the curriculum) is hard, although you may feel as if you are demonstrating admirable empathy, you may in fact be doing a great deal of damage by predisposing your pupils against the very thing you want them to engage with. As Eliot writes:

> difficulty may be caused by the reader having been told, or having suggested to himself that the poem is going to prove difficult. The ordinary reader, when warned against the obscurity of a poem, is apt to be thrown into a state of consternation very unfavourable to poetic receptivity.

(Ibid.)

Activity 8.3

Eliot on poetry

Think about Eliot's views of poetry, then respond to the following questions:

- How do Eliot's views relate to your own experiences of studying poetry?
- What types of poetry do you find easiest to relate to?
- What types of poetry did you (do you still) find it difficult to relate to?
- Why do you think this is?
- What do you think Eliot means by 'poetic receptivity'?

The following sections of this chapter go on to explore a number of different practical ways in which you could seek to enliven pupils' experiences of reading and studying poetry. Ways in which you can make it more of an enjoyable experience. To succeed in this it is important that you provide pupils with experiences of poetry that are not merely pragmatic. The repeated image of a class of pupils being dragged lesson by lesson through the GCSE anthology of set poems, applying the repeated formula of onomatopoeia, alliteration, simile, metaphor, assonance, etc. is as soul destroying for you to teach as it is for your pupils to experience.

Engaged personal exploration that creates interest and enthusiasm is at the heart of successful poetry teaching. If nothing else it demonstrates that you as a teacher are creatively involved with the poetry and enthusiastic about it, rather than viewing the text simply as the object of rather dry analysis. Not that teaching analysis in poetry lessons is not important – on the contrary, it is very important that pupils do learn the art of literary analysis – but your approach to analysis as a teacher needs to be varied and creative if pupils are to have an enriching rather than a damaging experience of poetry and are to see that analysis emerges from creativity.

SUBJECT KNOWLEDGE

As you begin your teaching career it would be a good idea to audit your knowledge of poetry against the proposed NC lists (http://www.education.gov.uk/schools/teachingandlearning/curriculum/secondary/b00199101/english). The NC requires that during KS3 and KS4 pupils study poetry in four categories:

- pre-twentieth century (two to be studied);
- twentieth century (two to be studied);
- contemporary;
- other cultures and traditions.

Other important documents to consult are the examination specifications for GCSE and A Level, which will provide lists of authors and texts set for study at these levels. These can be found on the websites of the respective examination boards as follows:

- AQA – http://www.aqa.org.uk;
- Edexcel – http://www.edexcel.org.uk;
- OCR – http://www.ocr.org.uk;
- WJEC – http://www.wjec.co.uk.

All teachers have areas to develop within their subject knowledge for teaching (see Chapter 2). Lack of detailed knowledge in a specific area should not be seen as a weakness, but rather as an exciting challenge. Similarly, knowledge in a particular area should not be taken for granted, but should be challenged for its appropriateness within the particular context of teaching. Complacency leads to poor teaching, whereas creative engagement with new matter for teaching often leads to engaged and exciting teaching and learning. That is why it is important for teachers regularly to update teaching materials and to take on the challenge each year of teaching things they have not taught before.

As you begin to think about your teaching of poetry, it is important, therefore, to think carefully about what you know and what you do not know. What aspects of poetry have you studied and are you comfortable with? How does knowledge in these areas relate to the demands of teaching poetry in the secondary school context? What aspects of teaching poetry are you less familiar with? How will you set about developing knowledge in these areas? These are questions which you, as a teacher, should be regularly asking yourself. The following auditing activity will provide a useful starting point in this process.

Activity 8.4

Auditing your poetry knowledge

1. List of major pre-twentieth century poets

The following list is a compulsory list. This *does not* mean that teachers can only teach poets from this list to their pupils – a mistake teachers often make early in their careers – but that at least two from the list must be included in your teaching.

Arnold, Blake, Charlotte Brontë, Emily Brontë, Elizabeth Browning, Robert Browning, Burns, Byron, Chaucer, Clare, Coleridge, Donne, Dryden, Gray,

---

Activity 8.4 *continued*

Herbert, Herrick, Hopkins, Keats, Marlowe, Marvell, Milton, Pope, Rossetti, Shakespeare (sonnets), Shelley, Spenser, Swift, Tennyson, Vaughan, Wordsworth, Wyatt.

- Identify as fully as possible your familiarity with the poetry of these authors. Do not worry if you have not read much (or anything) by all of them. The purpose of this is to identify constructive areas for development.
- Are there other pre-twentieth century poets you would like to teach as well as those listed here? Who are they, and how could you build teaching of them into programmes of study?

2. Examples of major poets after 1900

This is *not* a compulsory list, but rather identifies examples of suitable poets for study.

K. Amis, Auden, Douglas, Eliot, Frost, Heaney, Hughes, Jennings, Joyce, Larkin, Lawrence, Owen, Plath, Sassoon, Smith, Dylan Thomas, Edward Thomas, R. S. Thomas, Yeats.

- Again, identify as fully as possible your familiarity with the poetry of these authors.
- In addition, add the names of any other poets you think would merit study or you would like to teach.

3. Contemporary poets and poets from other cultures

This is *not* a compulsory list, but rather identifies examples of suitable poets for study.

Armitage, Causley, Clarke, Duffy, Fanthorpe, Haddon, Harrison, Henri, Lochhead, McGough, Mitchell, Rosen, Shapcott.

- Which other contemporary poets and poets from other cultures would you consider to be of significant literary merit? Devise your own lists.

On the basis of your audit and thinking, draw up a target reading list so that you can begin developing a wider range of poets you can draw on in your teaching. You should also include books on poetry if you feel that this is an area where you need to develop a deeper understanding.

USING ILLUSTRATIONS

This is a very useful technique for you to employ in a wide range of contexts in teaching English. It appeals to pupils' visual intelligence, but it does much more than that alone. It is important to remember that one of the most important tools in a writer's armoury is imagery – the process by which he/she uses words to paint a picture. The use of images to assist pupils in (re)creating meaning is therefore obvious. Images can be a powerful tool in helping pupils to unlock the meaning of the poetry they are studying. It is important to consider their use carefully, however, as they can both open and limit pupils' responses to the text.

Activity 8.5

Use of images

Use Figure 8.1 to record ways in which you believe the use of images can both open and limit pupils' responses.

Use of visual images	
Open responses	Limit responses

Figure 8.1 Use of images

The impact of visual images is best explored through another activity.

Activity 8.6

'London'

Read Blake's famous poem 'London' in a text only version, then jot down your initial responses to the poem. Here are some thoughts for starters.

- How is the city peopled?
- What locations does he emphasise?
- What about the sounds of the city?
- What are the most striking images?
- What vocabulary issues most strike you?
- What about the poem's rhyme and rhythm?
- What impression do these factors combine to give you of the city of London?

This is the way that most of you – if you have studied the poem before – will have encountered it, and it is probably the way that most pupils encounter it. Blake, however, never published the poem in a text only version. The poems of the *Songs of Innocence and of*

Experience were produced as engravings, within the context of which the poem was placed or framed. Look at a variety of the published versions of the poem in its illustrated context. Go to http://www.blakearchive.org/exist/blake/archive/work.xq?workid=songsie, which provides an excellent range of the available versions of the *Songs of Innocence and Experience*.

Activity 8.7

Images and reading

Look back to your earlier responses to the 'text only' poem:

- How does the illustration change your interpretation of what the poem is about?
- How does the image relate (or not relate) to the verbal content of the poem?

And now let's think more abstractly. While Blake's *Songs* is in a sense an unusual example, as he conceived of the images and the words as equal makers of meaning, the general principles of using images in the teaching of poetry hold true. The presence of the visual image simultaneously adds to and subtracts from the reader's experience of the poem. Whilst the image can add layers of meaning to the words, it can also take from the reader the validity of certain interpretations or force them in the direction of others.

Test this out. Look again at the two versions of 'London':

- What does the illustration add to your original reading of the poem?
- What does it take away from it?

If you are interested in looking into Blake's illustrations further, a large archive of his illustrated books and other illustrations can be found at http://www.blakearchive.org.

The French artist and illustrator Gustave Doré is another interesting and useful example to look into. Most famously he illustrated Coleridge's *Rime of the Ancient Mariner*, but also produced illustrations, amongst others, for works by Byron, Milton, Hood, Tennyson, Shakespeare and Poe.

Illustrations do not have to be works of art, however. Providing visual stimuli related to poems can be very useful to pupils in illuminating their understanding. Bringing a picture of a yam (or indeed a real yam) into the classroom while teaching 'Not My Business' by Niyi Osundare, would introduce pupils to an unfamiliar object. Pupils studying the works of Owen, Sassoon or a range of other war poets could be shown illustrations, as in Activity 8.8, to help them imagine something of the conditions experienced by men living and fighting in the trenches during World War I.

Activity 8.8

Images as context and stimulus

Go online and draw together a set of still images relating to World War I. These might be paintings or photographs.

Activity 8.8 *continued*

List some of the ways that you could use these images to help pupils understand something of the context surrounding the writings of the war poets.

You could use these pictures as a stimulus for pupils to write their own poetry of war. Think about how you might employ these images to do this.

Now have a go at Activity 8.9, where you will relate the idea of using images specifically to some poems and poets you may teach.

Activity 8.9

Building an illustrations bank

Instead of requiring pupils to respond to their reading of poetry by writing, why not ask them to respond by building an annotated image bank. You may even give them a selection of poems and/or poets to choose from. They may opt for specific illustrations of the poems or poet they are studying (like Doré's illustrations of Coleridge or Winterhouse's depiction of Tennyson's 'The Lady of Shallot'), or they may look to build up collages of images to try to capture the kaleidoscopic spirit of Blake's 'London'. Alternatively, they may provide illustrations that help them visualise unfamiliar terrains or places. The images they choose may be still or moving. Each image should be accompanied by a short piece of writing, or a short explanation if their responses are being presented to the class.

TEACHING POETIC TERMS

The teaching of poetic terms is a significant issue in relation to the teaching of poetry. Teachers often seem to feel pressure to introduce pupils very quickly to a wide range of specific terminology, as if this were a magic wand to wave at a text which will suddenly unlock all its secrets. The reality is that the teaching of poetic terminology is not a straightforward matter. Many pupils, when approaching poetry in the classroom, find themselves bombarded with specific and often unhelpful technical terminology which they are expected to apply meaningfully within their responses to texts. A sudden and often relatively unexplained barrage of jargon can be both disorientating and debilitating, damaging pupils' response not only to the poem in question, but to poetry in general. The complex metalanguage of poetic analysis can serve not to open the gate of the wonderful world of poetry, but can firmly slam it shut, confirming that poetry is unapproachable and hard. Perhaps this was even your experience.

As a pedagogic principle, it is important that you are sensitive and appropriate in the way you approach the teaching of technical terms. The ability to recognise onomatopoeia or alliteration actually does very little to enable pupils to respond to poetry, and tends, if you are not careful, to reduce the act of analysis to a rather futile naming of parts. What is far more useful is the ability to recognise the power individual words and phrases have within the context of any given poem and how these words and phrases impact upon a reader. The ability to apply specific names to the means by which poets achieve this is obviously important, and you need systematically to guide pupils towards this goal, but is not in itself always useful. The naming of names, in other words, should never be an end in itself, a trap that pupils (and teachers) can all too easily be lured into. Rather, it is essential to explore how a poet's use of particular poetic devices enhances meaning within the text under consideration. It is important, in other words, to recognise that clearly conveyed conceptual understanding is more important than the application of technical terminology.

This can easily be illustrated. Look at the following two examples, drawn from pupils' work on 'London'. Which conveys the more useful and sophisticated response?

Response 1

In the final verse of the poem Blake makes good use of an oxymoron when he talks about the 'marriage-hearse'.

Response 2

When Blake talks about the 'marriage-hearse' in the last verse of the poem he shows us the death and destruction that threaten the lives of people in the city.

The first pupil has correctly identified the poetic device Blake has employed, but has done nothing to explore how this contributes to her understanding of the poem. It would be easy to take the application of the term 'oxymoron' as proof of deep understanding. In reality, however, it does nothing to prove that the pupil knows why this is significant, which is much more important. The second pupil, on the other hand, has named no names. No oxymorons here. He has, however, offered a much more sophisticated response. It is clear from what he has written how the words on the page have affected his understanding, and that understanding is clearly displayed. As a rule of thumb remember that reasons without terms are more useful than terms without reasons. As in any aspect of learning, the appropriate use of metalanguage is empowering, providing learners with a useful means of expressing their understanding. It is important to think carefully about when it is appropriate to introduce such terminology, why it is being introduced, and how this can be done so as to enhance pupils' learning experience.

Activity 8.10

Use of literary terms

The following is a list of useful literary terms without definitions. Think carefully about how you would seek to define each of these terms for your pupils.

allegory, alliteration, allusion, alternating rhyme, antithesis, assonance, bathos, caesura, cliché, colloquial, connotation, contextuality, couplet, didactic, enjambment, end-stopped line, feminine rhyme, genre, hyperbole, imagery, internal rhyme, irony, juxtaposition, litotes, lyric poetry, metaphor, metre, onomatopoeia, oxymoron, paradox, pathetic fallacy, pathos, persona, personification, plurality, prosody, pun, quatrain, register, rhyme, rhythm, simile, stereotype, symbolism, synecdoche, theme, tone, triplet.

- Are there any other terms you would add to this list?
- Which terms would you introduce at Key Stage 3?
- Which would you add at Key Stage 4?
- Which would you introduce at A Level?
- Find examples you would use to illustrate these terms.

USING MUSIC

There are obvious connections between the teaching of poetry and music through the use of songs. Blake calls his most famous work *Songs of Innocence and of Experience*. Donne published a volume entitled *Songs and Sonets*. The word 'lyric' applies equally to songs and poetry and has its root in the Greek word λυρικός, which indicated that a poem was to be recited or sung to the accompaniment of a lyre. As a teacher, therefore, you may well wish to make use of such obvious connections in your teaching. Especially as so many pupils who claim to hate poetry will in the same breath express their love of music.

There are several contemporary poets, such as John Hegley, Benjamin Zephaniah and Lemn Sisay who follow the tradition of writing poetry to be performed to music. Songwriters such as Bob Dylan, Simon and Garfunkel, Lennon and McCartney and others are often regarded as poets who chose to write songs, and their lyrics repay close study with the added attraction of music. Recordings of all of these are easy to come by. On a more overtly literary note, Shakespeare wrote songs to be performed within his plays, all of which have been recorded and are readily available. In addition, countless thousands of poems have been set to music by composers covering a wide range of musical genres from classical to jazz-punk and beyond.

Activity 8.11

Poetry and music

Consider the following:

- How could you use song lyrics as a way into teaching other poetry? Would you approach the teaching of song differently to the teaching of 'straight' poetry? If so, how?
- What particular logistical and/or classroom management issues would you face if you choose to use music in teaching poetry?
- Look again at the poets you identified in Activity 8.9. Do a search to see what musical resources you could find to feed into your teaching here.
- How could you use music as a stimulus to poetry writing?

WRITING POETRY

Writing poetry creates great understanding in pupils that they cannot gain solely through academic study. The repeated scenario of pupils around the country being dragged kicking and screaming through the GCSE poetry anthology looking for endless examples of onomatopoeia, alliteration, rhyme, assonance, metaphor, simile and so on, ensures that many pupils do not enjoy engaging with poetry. Such an approach is also of limited value in terms of developing deep understanding. Far more effective in allowing your pupils to engage deeply with these devices and concepts is to provide them with structured opportunities to use them for themselves.

DEVELOPING POETRY ANTHOLOGIES

Developing themed anthologies of poetry (and including other relevant texts, such as prose extracts, non-fiction, drama extracts, literary criticism, etc.) can be an exciting and interesting way of approaching poetry. Alternatively, pupils can be encouraged to devise their own anthologies around set themes or issues (e.g. animals, festivals, places, objects), drawing on poems by published authors but also including poems and other writings of their own. This gives pupils a creative way to interact with the writings of others. With the desktop publishing facilities available in most schools these can now also be produced to a high standard, and many pupils find the production of their work for 'real' audiences very motivating.

Activity 8.12

Devising anthologies

Devise your own anthologies. These will be a very useful resource for you as you begin your teaching career. The anthologies can include not only poems, but also related writings (such as prose, non-fiction, criticism, etc.) depending upon group and purpose.

    Choose one or more of the following themes and create your own anthologies for teaching: animals; war; horror; love; transport; sport; festivals; places; objects; buildings; famous people; etc.

Provide opportunities for pupils to write for 'real' audiences, not only for their teacher. Spending the time to develop in-house publications within the school or for sale to parents can really inspire young writers who rise admirably to the challenge. There are also many young writer competitions and publications which you as a teacher can encourage your pupils to enter.

CONCLUSIONS

Teaching poetry can be one of the great pleasures of the English classroom. By their nature, poems tend to be short and manageable texts that lend themselves well to teaching in single lessons or in short sequences of lessons. This offers you as a teacher the potential to be imaginative and widely eclectic in your approaches to teaching. By the same token, it can also lead to the development of repetitive and uninspiring formulae – especially where the added pressure of GCSE examinations or GCE A Level modules is added into the equation. The importance, for pupils and teachers alike, of variety should not be underestimated, however.

RECOMMENDED READING

Eliot, T. S. (1932) *Selected Essays*. London: Faber & Faber.
Fry, S. (2005) *The Ode Less Travelled*. London: Hutchinson.
Heaney, S. (1980) *Preoccupations*. London: Faber & Faber.
Hughes, T. (2008) *Poetry in the Making: A Handbook for Writing and Teaching*. London: Faber.
Hyland, P. (1992) *Getting into Poetry*. Tarset: Bloodaxe Books.
Naylor, A. and Wood, A. B. (2012) *Teaching Poetry*. London: Routledge.
Sidney, P. (1966) *An Apologie for Poetrie*. Oxford: Oxford University Press.

Chapter 9   Teaching reading

CARMEL KELLETT AND LINDA VARLEY

In this chapter you will consider:

- how to teach a whole class reader;
- principles for teaching reading;
- how to establish a reading community;
- a range of contexts for teaching reading;
- a range of texts for study at KS3 and KS4;
- a range of strategies for teaching reading.

INTRODUCTION

Whether teaching KS3 or KS4 it is essential that you have read any book and know it well in its entirety before you start teaching it. You need to have thought out what ideas you want to explore and think about how these will be addressed as you progress through the text. This will help when planning homework or silent reading, since you will know which chapters are more straightforward and can be read independently. Most of all, have the confidence to engage in active learning methods because what you want to achieve is the creation of a reading community within your classroom.

For many pupils one of the only opportunities they will have to experience sustained reading is in the English classroom: this may be a single text, a group of short stories, a selection of poems, a drama or non-fiction text chosen by the teacher (or an exam board) which is read by all of the pupils at the same time. So it is important for you to ensure that the text is taught in a way that engages the pupils and turns reluctant readers into part of that reading community. If this is to be their only experience of reading fiction then try and make it a pleasurable one.

PUPILS AS READERS

The Children's Laureate (2003–5), Michael Morpurgo, argues that 'If children are to become readers for life, they must first love stories.' This underpins the ideals of the NC (which intends that *pupils learn to become enthusiastic and critical readers*) and it is expected that pupils will have a clear understanding of the *author's craft*. However, before you go into schools to transform everyone into avid readers you do need to be prepared to meet the challenge of pupils who consider reading as an alien pastime and are consequently very reluctant to engage in the reading process.

'Children's enjoyment of reading has declined since 1998 ... children are now less likely to enjoy reading stories, poems and information books.' This was the conclusion of a national survey to investigate children's reading enjoyment organised by the National Foundation for Educational Research (NFER) which tracked the reading habits of approximately 5000 children in 1998 and 2003. This finding was supported in 2003 when the Progress for International Reading Literacy Study (PIRLS) presented the results of an internationally comparative reading study from 35 countries. The report concluded that 'although the reading skills of 10 year old pupils in England compared well with those pupils in other countries, they read less frequently for pleasure and were less interested in reading than elsewhere.'

CHOOSING TEXTS

Research undertaken with primary school teachers (UKLA [2006] Teachers as Readers: Phase 1 Research Report) found that 73 per cent had read for pleasure during the last month. When asked to list six good children's writers, 46 per cent were able to name six, but in terms of books chosen for children, the range was severely limited, with many of the books cited being those which teachers had read themselves as children.

Activity 9.1

Teachers' reading

Read the UKLA report to understand the key issues raised and conduct your own survey of peers who are secondary English teachers or trainees. You may wish to download the full questionnaire or use the 5 key questions given below: (http://www.ukla.org/research/research_projects_in_progress/ukla_research_on_teachers_as_readers/)

Q1: List current reading in the last month.
Q2: What category of reading was this?

    1   Pleasure – what genre?
    2   Children's/teenage fiction?
    3   Newspapers and magazines?

Q3: What is the most important book you have ever read?
Q4: What is your favourite childhood book?
Q5: List 6 'good' children's writers.

The survey questions in Activity 9.1 were completed by 20 PGCE Secondary English trainees in July 2011 and 90 per cent reported that they read for pleasure but the limited range of KS3 reading followed the same pattern of the 2006 survey, with most citing their own teenage reading. The following advice was given by one NQT, Victoria:

> Read as many Key Stage 3 novels as you can so that when a pupil says they have enjoyed a book you can recommend another that is similar. If a pupil tells me they like Philip Pullman's fantasy quest *Northern Lights* I suggest they read Anthony Horowitz's *Raven's Gate* which is another sinister supernatural adventure.

Let us assume that as the class teacher you have autonomy over the selection of the class reader. In an ideal situation you would be able to say, 'I love X and want to teach it,' and there would be a full class set in the stockroom. In reality you will go into the stockroom and find out what is available (which may also involve negotiation with colleagues); you sometimes have to balance what the pupils may enjoy with your own knowledge of a text. Sometimes unlikely choices work well. You may have to choose a book you do not know, with rapid reading on your part, or the available text (such as Roald Dahl's *Charlie and the Chocolate Factory*) may not seem the best option.

Figure 9.1 lists class fiction readers that were used by eight English teachers as NQTs, and there are some surprising selections for both Key Stages (the number in brackets indicates the number out of the eight NQTs who used the text).

You may be surprised to see Charles Dickens' *Great Expectations* as a KS3 text, but judicious selection of extracts means that the text is very approachable, and pupils develop familiarity with the old-fashioned language. Once the pupils have 'tuned in' to Dickens' language, then they can take the whole of *A Christmas Carol*. In the same way George Eliot's *Silas Marner* may seem old-fashioned but this tale of an outsider of society who is redeemed by a young child resonates with young adults.

Fiction, however, is only part of the story. Pupils are also expected to read in a range of other genres. The lists in Figures 9.2, 9.3 and 9.4 have been compiled by PGCE trainees and NQTs and the choices reflect the ability level of the class and the greater opportunity to explore non-fiction reading at KS3.

The poetry selected represents a range of poetic forms and genres, although narrative poems and ballads seem to have been the most popular at KS3. The demands of GCSE have dictated the selection of poetry studied at KS4.

A pattern that has emerged in the drama studied is that extracts of Shakespeare's plays may be looked at for KS3, but by KS4, the whole play is studied, some citing their use for Controlled Assessments at GCSE. In this genre there is a far wider range of plays read at KS4 than at KS3.

KS3	KS4
Holes – Louis Sachar (3)	*Of Mice and Men* – John Steinbeck (6)
The Boy in the Striped Pyjamas – John Boyne (3)	*Lord of the Flies* – William Golding (3)
Noughts and Crosses – Malorie Blackman (2)	*Pride and Prejudice* – Jane Austen (3)
Private Peaceful – Michael Morpurgo (2)	*To Kill a Mockingbird* – Harper Lee (2)
Skellig – David Almond (2)	*Animal Farm* – George Orwell
Stone Cold – Robert Swindells (2)	*Silas Marner* – George Eliot
A Christmas Carol – Charles Dickens	*Stone Cold* – Robert Swindells
A Series of Unfortunate Events – Lemony Snicket	
Abomination – Robert Swindells	
Animal Farm – George Orwell	
Brother in the Land – Robert Swindells	
Bumface – Morris Gleitzman	
Cinderella (Joseph Jacobs' version, Charles Perrault version and a modern native American version)	
Face – Benjamin Zephaniah	
Harry Potter and the Philosopher's Stone – J. K. Rowling	
Lord of the Flies – William Golding	
Mortal Engines – Philip Reeve	
Proven Guilty – Jim Butcher	
Raven's Gate – Anthony Horowitz	
Stormbreaker – Anthony Horowitz	
The Black Book of Secrets – F. E. Higgins	
The Defender – Alan Gibbons	
Two weeks with the Queen – Morris Gleitzman	
Great Expectations (extracts) – Charles Dickens	
Twilight (extracts) – Stephenie Meyer	
Witch Child – Celia Rees	

Figure 9.1 Fiction texts

KS3	KS4
Diary Anne Frank's Diary Diary accounts of 9/11 Diary entries from The Freedom Writers Diary Speeches Obama – various Martin Luther King – I have a dream Travel writing Bill Bryson – various Other Olympics – leaflets, videos, general articles Science articles	Autobiography *I know why the caged bird sings* – Maya Angelou

Figure 9.2 Non-fiction texts

KS3	KS4
Browning, Robert – 'The Pied Piper of Hamelin' Coleridge, Samuel Taylor – 'The Rime of the Ancient Mariner' De La Mare, Walter – 'The Listeners' Eliot, T. S. – 'Macavity – The Mystery Cat' Hardy, Thomas – 'Under the Waterfall' Henri, Adrian – 'Without You' McGough, Roger – 'The Lesson' McGough, Roger – 'The Way Things Are' Tennyson, Alfred Lord – 'Godiva' Tennyson, Alfred Lord – 'Mariana' Tennyson, Alfred Lord – 'The Lady of Shallot' Wright, Luke – 'The Ballad of Fat Josh' Zephaniah, Benjamin – 'The British' Zephaniah, Benjamin – 'Talking Turkeys!'	Alvi, Moniza – 'Unknown Girl' Angelou, Maya – 'Still I Rise' Armitage, Simon – 'About His Person' Armitage, Simon – 'Harmonium' Auden, W. H. – 'Ode' Auden, W. H. – 'O where are you going' Dharker, Imtiaz – 'Blessing' Duffy, Carol Ann – 'Havisham' Duffy, Carol Ann – 'Medusa' Duffy, Carol Ann – 'War Photographer' Duffy, Carol Ann – 'Valentine' Hardy, Thomas – 'The Man He Killed' Hardy, Thomas – 'Under the Waterfall' Heaney, Seamus – 'Personal Helicon' King, William – 'The Beggar Woman' McGough, Roger – 'Icarus Allsorts' Owen, Wilfred – 'Dulce et Decorum Est' Owen, Wilfred – 'Exposure'

Figure 9.3 Poetry texts

KS3	KS4
Shakespeare *Macbeth* (extract) *Much Ado About Nothing* *The Tempest* *The Winter's Tale* (extract) *Twelfth Night* Other *40 Short Plays* – Ann Cartwright *Frankenstein* – adapted by Philip Pullman *Our Day Out* – Willy Russell	Shakespeare *As You Like It* *Macbeth* *Romeo and Juliet* *The Taming of the Shrew* Other *The History Boys* – Alan Bennett *Hedda Gabler* – Henrik Ibsen *My Mother Never Said I Should* – Charlotte Keatley *The Crucible* – Arthur Miller *An Inspector Calls* – J. B. Priestley *Blood Brothers* – Willy Russell *Educating Rita* – Willy Russell

Figure 9.4 Drama texts

There are a number of factors that you will need to consider in the selection of texts as a class reader, but the key component is the pupils you will be teaching. What is the composition of the class? Are there more males than females? What is their level of maturity? Do they have any preferred interests? How will you sell the story to them? There is not a perfect answer; the key thing is that you need to know your class. However, if you have more males than females you may wish to avoid *The Diary of Anne Frank* or Jane Austen's *Pride and Prejudice*. The level of maturity of the class may mean that you would avoid Maya Angelou's biographical account of her early life, with its frank account of racial prejudice and childhood abuse. However, that very content allows for an exploration of moral and personal issues as pupils empathise with the writer's experiences. It can also be seen that the same book (e.g. George Orwell's *Animal Farm* in Figure 9.2 or *Macbeth* in Figure 9.4) was used successfully in both KS3 and KS4 classes. Here the NQTs knew the composition of their classes and judged at which stage they would be receptive to looking at an account of a totalitarian regime or a Shakespeare play.

Activity 9.2

Your reading at school

Consider your own experiences at school. Think of a range of ways in which teachers introduced you to the class reader. Did these approaches enthuse you? What did you gain from them?

WAYS INTO TEXTS

It would be very easy to begin a class reader by reading from page one. Yet prior to reading the text it is useful to incorporate some tasks that establish it. This allows you to launch the text in an exciting way that hopefully gains the interest of the pupils. And for some texts it is useful to provide some background information to support understanding of character and plot. *Private Peaceful* by Michael Morpurgo is a good example to consider. This is about a soldier who is looking back on his life in the trenches of World War I. For this class reader context provides a good starting point. Pupils studying this text could be shown images or DVDs of the conditions endured by the men during this war. This provides information which is useful for them in order to empathise with the characters. You may also wish to combine the teaching of the novel with a study of a range of relevant poetry, non-fiction and wartime propaganda.

Drama, especially improvisation, is an enjoyable and empathetic way to engage with issues and characters. *Holes* by Louis Sachar is a story of an innocent boy sentenced to serve his sentence in a brutal detention camp in America and is set the menial task of digging holes. A variety of scenarios related to bullying and decision-making could be introduced that would allow pupils this opportunity.

'Macavity' by T. S. Eliot is a popular poem to use in the classroom. The focus is on a cat called Macavity who is a master criminal who commits lots of crimes but is too clever to be caught. There are many interesting ways in which the poem may be introduced: creating a crime scene prior to reading the poem engages the pupils as well as allowing them to use many skills of inference and deduction by analysing the clues from the poem. There is also a musical based on the poem called *Cats*; selected highlights could be shown to provide a visual stimulus and a starting point for discussion on the characters.

Skellig by David Almond is a fantasy tale about a boy's relationship with a bird-like angel that changes his outlook on life. The story also focuses on his friendship with Mina, a young girl who happens to be home-schooled. Blake's poem 'The Schoolboy' (which is referred to in the text) could be introduced prior to reading to provide a way into ideas that Almond deals with.

'The Lady of Shallot' by Lord Alfred Tennyson is an Arthurian narrative poem set in the medieval period. There is a variety of both visual and audio readings of the poem that can be utilised prior to reading the poem. This ensures that an effective reading can be heard first time that engages the pupils and maintains their interest especially as they will be introduced to some unfamiliar vocabulary.

A favourite approach of many experienced teachers is the exploration of the front cover and blurb of the text they are covering (or indeed a comparison of a range of covers and blurbs that have been used for the same texts in different times and places) which allows pupils to engage in prediction exercises. This also allows classes an insight into the ways in which their reading of particular texts might be influenced by (even manipulated by) publishers' choices.

All of these approaches can be utilised but you need to think very carefully about the most effective way to introduce the text: what do the pupils need to ensure that they can engage with the issues and characters? Do they need some contextual information? Would some role play tasks allow them to empathise with character? If the pupils are excited about starting to read the text then you have successfully launched it. The question now is how to sustain the enthusiasm?

Creative assessment

Reading can be used as a vehicle for assessing not only the reading itself but also writing and speaking and listening.

1   One way to assess reading is to create a 'book club' approach, encouraging class members to read a range of texts and to report (and sell the book) to their peers. Peers can question and challenge and a vote is taken on which was the most effective in encouraging others to read (as you will be aware, there are attendant speaking and listening skills that can be assessed at the same time).

2   A text can be adapted in written form (characters, plot and setting presented for film or television) or transformed (a prequel or sequel, for example; or from the perspective of a different protagonist). The advantage of doing this is that pupils gain insight and deeper understanding of a text.

3   Drama-based tasks can be used to assess pupils' understanding of character. The main focus may be some form of role play, news report, hot seating or chat show yet it is the actual 'talk' taking place in the groups prior to the performance that is invaluable. Here is an opportunity to explore ideas and issues related to the characters.

HOW TO READ THE TEXT

This is probably the most problematic decision you will have to make. You know that you only have a fixed amount of time to read the whole text (normally 6–7 weeks), but you want to spend time exploring active learning approaches that engage the pupils and support understanding of the issues and characters. Figure 9.5 shows a variety of methods that can be used in and out of the classroom. As you can see, each approach has merits but also pitfalls. What does this tell us? By utilising a variety of approaches you should at least cater for most pupils. Again think back to your own experiences. How did you feel when you were asked to read aloud? Were you one of those pupils who dreaded the thought? You will find many of these pupils in your classroom.

When you want to allow pupils an opportunity to participate in reading, you could adopt the group reading approach. It does not even require the whole chapter to be read by all; instead selected parts could be allocated to each group. This may, however, lead to some difficulties of continuity for pupils working on later sections of the text and you will need to ensure that pupils are provided with sufficient information to access and respond to the section of the text they are given to read. To overcome this, you could set a

Strategies	Advantages	Disadvantages
Read around the class	This is very inclusive as it provides every pupil with an opportunity to read aloud even for a short period. It gives everyone a chance to develop their reading skills. It can promote confidence amongst passive learners.	It may become a monotonous exercise, particularly if some of the reading lacks quality. Concentration levels of other pupils may wane if they are not engaged with the text. Some pupils may be reluctant to read aloud and could even refuse.
Selected readers	Effective readers chosen by the teacher (either volunteers or teacher-selected) can bring a text to life and engage all members of the class. Other pupils can hear good models for reading on a whole-class basis. If selected readers are numbered there is continuity to the reading.	This can exclude other pupils from participating in the exercise. If volunteers are requested, the quality of the reading will vary.
Teacher reading	A teacher who reads eloquently with plenty of animation can bring a text to life and engage all pupils.	It excludes active participation from the pupils. An ineffective reading could lead to concentration levels waning and it is difficult to monitor and admonish unacceptable behaviour.
Group reading in class	This enables the less confident readers an opportunity to read in a supportive group. The teacher can work closely with small groups on sections of the text and hence can monitor more effectively. Pupils can work independently on sections of the text as long as there is some structured guidance. Experimenting with different methods of reading is viable.	The classroom may become quite noisy and individuals could struggle to listen attentively.
Individual silent reading	This allows pupils to read at their own pace.	Some pupils may struggle to concentrate in the uncomfortable surroundings of the classroom. Lower ability pupils may struggle with comprehension and aspects of the vocabulary.
Individual reading at home	This allows pupils to read at their own pace in comfortable surroundings.	It may be that your school does not allow pupils to take books home (they may be lost; forgotten etc and the school loses whole class sets). Some pupils may struggle without the support of their teacher or peers. It is difficult for the teacher to monitor the reading.
Teacher reads narration and the spoken voices of characters are given to designated pupils	There is a sense of dramatic performance. Pupils learn the conventions of speech punctuation and the variety of forms that can signal spoken dialogue in written texts. It requires full concentration from the pupils. It can allow even the less confident to contribute since the teacher can signal 'X is a very small part' to encourage reluctant volunteer readers.	There can be a disjointed reading if pupils miss their cues. The text needs to have sufficient spoken dialogue for this to work effectively; careful selection is important.

Figure 9.5 Reading the text

homework task to read the whole chapter and the extract-based task could be a consolidation or extension activity. Each group could feedback their interpretation of the chapter in a variety of creative ways such as tableaux, role play or mime. This offers a less scary experience for less confident readers and it allows you to monitor individuals. You may need to book a large space such as a drama hall as it can become quite noisy, or if this is not possible try and ensure that groups are not too close together within the classroom.

When approaching a more difficult section within a text or when a section is linked to the long term objectives then it is important that a good, clear reading is provided either by the teacher or effective readers within the classroom. You could, if you wished, find an audio version of the text. Otherwise a lacklustre reading could frustrate more able readers and could weaken the concentration of others, hindering comprehension. Remember, many of us still take pleasure from being read to.

One of the key issues is actually reading the whole text in the allotted time; this is often a concern for inexperienced teachers who may end up spending the last few lessons of the scheme of work reading the text in order to finish it. Reading some sections for homework is invaluable, but choose the sections carefully so that they are accessible to all pupils. Monitoring strategies and prompts need to be incorporated so that you are aware that the reading has taken place.

Activity 9.3

Supporting reading

Below is a list of example prompt activities that can support the reading of the pupils. Can you provide more examples from your own experiences?

- mind map
- character charts
- interviews with characters and the author
- chapter titles
- reading logs
- quizzes

HOW TO TEACH A TEXT

In this section we will use a worked example drawing on John Boyne's *The Boy in the Striped Pyjamas* where an innocent child's view of Auschwitz and the Holocaust is presented. As an English teacher, when addressing the NC strand *2.2 Reading for Meaning*, you will be expected to introduce your pupils to multimodal texts, and so this example will also incorporate discussion of the recent film adaptation of John Boyne's novel. In the NC, multimodal texts are defined as texts that:

> combine two or more modes of communication (e.g. written, aural and visual) to create meaning. Examples include the combination of words and images in a newspaper or magazine, the combination of words, images, video clips and sound on a website or CD-ROM, or the combination of images, speech and sound in moving-image texts.

The film adaptation of *The Boy in the Striped Pyjamas* provides a number of means of integrating film and text:

1   Book covers are chosen to illustrate the narrative, incorporating suggestions through the use of colour and pattern in the design. A film poster combines images with written text, designed to give audiences an introduction to a film and encourage them to go and see it. Discussion of the two different still visual representations offers a useful way in to thinking about the novel and the film.

2   The blurb on the back cover of the book gives an idea of the plot, characters and setting, although in the case of this blurb it is not as straightforward: *'The story of "The Boy in the Striped Pyjamas" is very difficult to describe. Usually we give some clues about the book on the cover, but in this case we think it would spoil the reading of the book.'* Film trailers serve somewhat the same function as book blurbs; key moments from the

film are put together with titles and music to persuade audiences to watch the film. Watching trailers can provide interesting opportunities for pupils to look at the style and setting of the film, to explore narrative and to consider the kind of audience for the film.

3   The first page (or first few pages) of the book can be compared to the film's opening sequence. Just as the opening of the book has to hook its readers, so the first few minutes of a film have a real influence on the way that the audience responds to what they see and hear. In the book, Boyne offers a puzzle (why is Maria packing?) and introduces the main characters, seen through Bruno's eyes. The film focuses on location, props and costume, as well as the way the scene has been shot, and this is supplemented by music and dialogue.

4   The contrast of innocence (or ignorance) with experience (or knowledge) is a key theme of the novel. This could be conveyed by presenting pupils with a variety of pictures (cartoons or photographs where there is ambiguity about the back story will work best) and asking them, in groups, to identify what is going on. They should come up with a range of responses which can lead on to discussion about how we make judgements and whether we often need more information to make accurate judgements. This offers an excellent introduction to the point in the film where Bruno sees something interesting outside his window and asks his mother about it. It will allow pupils to understand Bruno's perspective.

5   Context is something that may not be introduced until the pupils have grasped the implications of 'Out-With' (as Bruno naively mispronounces Auschwitz). It is at this point that pupils may be set to research Auschwitz, the Holocaust and the fate of the Jewish population of Cracow. This dawning implication is also developed through subtle clues in the film, such as the incident with Doctor Pavel when Bruno falls down and when Bruno discovers his friend Shmuel cleaning glasses in his house. Pupils can explore how the spoken (and unspoken) elements of multimodal texts (authorial craft) are used to create impact and meaning.

CONSIDERATIONS AT KS4

Once pupils embark on their GCSE English courses, the assessment of reading becomes more formal. Most exam boards require pupils to sit an external exam on a set prose text (or group of short stories) as well as poetry, drama and non-fiction texts with very clear assessment focuses (AFs) and a clearly defined mark scheme.

Many of the issues remain the same as at KS3 – choice of text, timescale and approaches to reading the text – but there is the added pressure of preparing pupils to tackle unseen questions under exam conditions. It would be very easy to take the formulaic approach of reading a chapter and then making notes but this can lead to low levels of engagement and enjoyment. Some of the active learning approaches utilised in KS3 should be utilised as well in KS4, as otherwise pupils can rapidly become disaffected.

Do not be afraid to use drama approaches with your year GCSE group (see Chapter 5 for a range of ideas): you may face some resistance at first but it can relate closely to a range of S&L assessment. *Of Mice and Men* by John Steinbeck is a popular choice of exam boards and teachers. It is the story of two migrant workers and their ill-fated search for the American Dream during the Great Depression of 1930s America. You could try role play tasks to explore characters' motivations or to see what is happening 'behind the scenes'; you could interview certain characters about their role in the unfolding events; or, for a more challenging task, try setting up a Jeremy Kyle style chat show where the characters can vent their frustrations and interact with one another. This format allows the pupils in groups to really engage with the characters and issues in a familiar setting both whilst planning the content of the drama and in performance. These approaches help pupils consolidate their understanding of characters and themes whilst providing an element of active and independent learning within the classroom.

The Crucible by Arthur Miller is another popular choice. The drama focuses on the Salem Witch Trials of the 1600s yet is an allegory for 1950s America. Again a range of role plays that explores characters' motivations and attitudes would really support pupils' understanding of the complexity of some of the characters. For a more challenging task, why not allow the pupils to create their own television or radio broadcast based on the hysteria created through trials both in Salem and in the McCarthy Communist 'witch hunts' of 1950s America.

Jonathan Swift's satirical article 'A Modest Proposal' of 1729 can be tackled through the use of collage and commentary. The piece mocks government attitudes to problems in Ireland at the time. Both the issues and the style of writing can be quite difficult for pupils. Allowing pupils the opportunity to create visual interpretations of the text can open up their understanding of Swift's imagery and this can feed back into their reading.

Pupils should be given as many opportunities as possible to discuss their reading. This process really allows them to influence their own learning and understanding of each other. Vygotsky (1978: 88) observes that language and talk support the development of thinking, so pupils who talk with others will learn to think and so 'grow into the intellectual life of those around them'. Class readers provide the opportunity to explore a range of contexts for talk, either between you and the pupils or between groups of pupils. Such dialogue about reading benefits pupils as they are encouraged to engage with their reading on a more personal and independent level and requires them to consider different interpretations of texts

Asking the right questions is central to the teaching and learning process. Bloom's (1956) 'taxonomy of educational objectives' is a useful classification to explore. He states that questions can be arranged into six levels of complexity starting with lower level, knowledge-based questions and moving towards more complex evaluation type questions. If you apply this to your own questioning you can ensure that pupils are being systematically challenged at appropriate levels and are exploring some of the complex elements of the texts they read critically, sensitively and in detail.

On a more practical level, there are key approaches that you can take:

- Pupils should be given the opportunity to look at past exam papers. The English department should have some readily available; if not, the website of your exam board will allow you to download examples. You can then see what areas have been targeted in previous exams; most exam boards tend not to consider the same theme or character in consecutive exams. By considering past questions you are giving your pupils an experience of the type of question asked which should give them confidence. Tackling past questions also provides you with evidence of pupils' knowledge and if any areas need further clarification.

- Allow pupils access to the mark scheme. Often it is useful to translate it into pupil-friendly language and then explore what they need to do to improve their own work. If they know what they have to do then this gives them confidence. You can use this in peer assessment; this forms a useful tool to assess learning and allows pupils to be part of the learning process.

- Film adaptations of novels can be a useful learning resource if utilised in the right way. If the film is shown when you have finished reading the novel and you feel that your pupils have a good grasp of plot, characters etc then this can be a consolidation exercise. However all adaptations will change certain aspects of source texts so it is important to ensure that you evaluate these changes, which can be a really useful approach to engage with higher order thinking. Some teachers may want to show the film early on, with no useful discussion to follow, but there is the danger that pupils will fail to differentiate effectively between the film and the book.

Activity 9.4

Film and reading

Consider your own thoughts about using film adaptations. Did you watch a film version of any texts studied? Was it a useful tool to support the text and your understanding of key issues and characters? How did the teacher use the film adaption? Evaluate the advantages and disadvantages of using film adaptations:

- prior to reading the text;
- during the reading of the text;
- after the reading of the text.

- Some questions will require pupils to have a good grasp of the social, cultural and historical contexts of texts. This needs to be covered initially when establishing the text but it is important that this is not covered as a discrete area but is fully integrated into the teaching of the whole text in order to embed understanding of its practical relevance.
- IGCSE English is a new exam that some schools have adopted. The main difference in Reading is the expectation of comparing texts. This does offer more challenge to your pupils. The approaches are still the same but more emphasis needs to be placed on the comparative aspects of texts (only specifically addressed through poetry at GCSE) which should not be left to the end of the reading but should be conistently addressed when tackling the second text. Pupils need to see the texts as linked units not two separate class readers.

CONCLUSIONS

This chapter has taken you through the process of teaching reading and offers a wide range of ideas for texts you could choose as the class reader. You will find it useful to look up these titles on the web where a summary of the plot and possible resources are likely to be available. These will help you to establish the text and to select how to read the text with your class. Advice is offered about how to approach a possible comparison of the text with a film version and it is important to remember that the practical approaches offered for KS3 texts are also applicable to KS4. The underpinning message is that you have the potential to instil a love of reading in your pupils and the power to create a community of readers within your classroom.

RECOMMENDED READING

Bloom, B. S. (1956) *Taxonomy of Educational Objectives, Handbook 1: Cognitive Domain*. London: Longman.

http://www.telegraph.co.uk/culture/books/3670594/100-books-every-child-should-read-An-introduction-by-Michael-Morpurgo.html

Mullis, I. V. S., Martin, M. O., Gonzalez, E. J. and Kennedy, A. (2003) *Pirls 2001 International Report: IEA's Study of Reading Literacy Achievement in Primary Schools*. Boston, USA.

Sainsbury, M. (2004) Childrens' Attitudes to Reading, *Literacy Today*, no. 38, pp. 16–17.

UKLA (United Kingdom Literary Association) (2006) Teachers as Readers: Phase 1 Research Report, available at http://www.ukla.org/research/research_projects_in_progress/ukla_research_on_teachers_as_readers/

Vygotsky, L. S. (1978) *Mind in Society: The Development of Higher Psychological Processes*. London: Harvard University Press.

Chapter 10 Teaching English Literature post-16

CAROL ATHERTON

In this chapter you will consider:

- important early issues when teaching A Level English Literature;
- the development of a short scheme of work to cover the first few weeks of an A Level course;
- a set of worked examples using Sylvia Plath's autobiographical novel *The Bell Jar*;
- how these methods could be adapted for use with a wide range of texts;
- pedagogy and its relationship with meaning in literary texts.

INTRODUCTION

What's your image of the perfect A Level English Literature classroom? Small groups? Enthusiastic readers? The chance to explore ideas? The lessons you look forward to above all others? People outside the teaching profession often imagine that teaching English Literature at A Level is the pinnacle of the English teacher's career. Their image of the A Level classroom (frequently coloured by nostalgia for their own A Level days) is of a place where highly-motivated students congregate to learn from inspirational teachers and encounter texts that will have a lasting impact on their lives. Some of us are lucky enough to experience this environment for real; and every year thousands of young people are challenged, stimulated and enthused by their study of English Literature at A Level, and by the teachers who guide them. Those of us who work in the post-16 sector, however, will know that A Level is also a highly pressurised experience for both teachers and students, dominated by rising class sizes and the ever-present demands of the assessment system. Beginning teachers often find the reality of A Level very difficult, particularly if they look back on their own A Level days as what Richard Jacobs (2010: 1) has described as an 'emotional high-point' when their love of the subject first crystallised. How, then, can you prepare yourself for the challenges of A Level teaching?

My first experience of post-16 teaching was like being dunked in a bath of icy water. I expected enthusiasm and eagerness: what I got was suspicion and indifference. I also had to contend with the arrogance of teenagers who had just got their GCSEs and saw me as just a newly qualified teacher: what did *I* know? It took a lot of lost sleep and a prolonged period of attrition before I moulded them into the kind of group I wanted them to be. I worked harder with that group than I have with any of my classes since then, and I can still remember how tough it was.

Teaching A Level English Literature is not always this difficult, but it certainly is not (as a Maths-teaching colleague of mine once jokingly claimed) a simple matter of 'sitting around reading books and talking about whether you like them or not'. Nor is it about the kind of subversive passion embodied by Robin Williams as John Keating in *Dead Poets' Society*, or, more recently, by Hector, the maverick teacher in Alan Bennett's *The History Boys*. In many ways, it is closer to the kind of experience described in a very different text: the children's book *That Rabbit Belongs to Emily Brown*, by Cressida Cowell and Neal Layton. Emily Brown is the owner of a much-loved toy rabbit called Stanley, with whom she explores the Amazon rainforest, travels to the South Pole and goes diving off the Great Barrier Reef. A spoiled and demanding young queen is envious of Emily, and sends her troops to kidnap Stanley, offering Emily a brand-new golden teddy bear in return. Emily, a very feisty little girl, is not impressed. She tells the queen: 'You take that horrid brand-new teddy bear and you play with him all day. Hold him very tight and be sure to have lots of adventures. And then maybe one day you will wake up with a real toy of your OWN.'

Emily Brown's advice holds true for anyone faced with a post-16 group for the first time. Granted, you should not hold them tight – that should go without saying – but you should certainly be prepared to put in an awful lot of effort to building your relationship with them, working out where they are in terms of their encounters with books and their thinking about literature, and considering how to get them to the next stage of their learning. Beginning teachers are often envious of the rapport that more experienced colleagues have with their post-16 classes. Richard Jacobs (2010: 2) has described the A Level teacher as a 'lightning conductor': a focal point for the energy generated by the meeting between challenging texts and impressionable young minds at a crucial stage of their intellectual development. This role is often performed apparently effortlessly, by teachers who might be remembered as lifelong influences. But in reality, vast amounts of work go into establishing and maintaining a successful relationship with an A Level group. Students start their post-16 courses less than a fortnight after getting their GCSE results: by the time they finish, they'll be ready to move on to higher education (HE) or employment. Teaching them involves establishing clear ground rules in the first heady weeks of post-compulsory study, nursing them through the transition from GCSE to the greater demands of their new courses, and then keeping them going through what will inevitably be a tough couple of years. Like making a brand-new golden teddy bear into your best friend, it's harder than it looks.

WAYS OF TEACHING; CONCEPTS OF 'MEANING'

There has been relatively little attention to the pedagogy of A Level: to the methods and philosophies that underpin successful A Level teaching. There is a tendency in some quarters to assume that teaching at A Level is somehow 'easier' than at KS3 or KS4, and that it can therefore be left to look after itself. Furthermore, the pressure of assessment means that some schools are reluctant to entrust their A Level groups to beginning teachers. It is possible to find yourself qualified to teach from 11 to 18 without ever having set foot in front of a post-16 class. It is hardly surprising, then, that many beginning teachers find their first A Level groups extremely intimidating – especially if they themselves have gone straight from school to university to ITE, and are therefore only a few years older than their students. Some cope by making their lessons excessively didactic, perhaps hoping to use a display of their own knowledge to shore up their authority. Others plump for the opposite approach, and try to lessen the gap between themselves and their students by being overly casual and non-directive. It should go without saying that neither approach is ideal. An entirely teacher-led methodology – described by Simon Gibbons (2010: 3) as involving '[the] heavily directed annotation of texts, large quantities of background notes, a standard whole class "seminar" style lesson structure, a reliance on students' note-taking skills' – can be intimidating and stifling, and suggests that 'meaning' is fixed and unchanging, offering students very little interpretive breathing-space. A sense, on the other hand, that meaning is completely subjective – that texts can mean 'whatever you want them to mean' – gives students almost unlimited freedom, but nevertheless risks 'coddl[ing them] into believing that their responses [are] valuable just because they are their own' (McCormick, 1994: 62), leaving them unprepared for the rigours of A Level assessment.

What is needed to resolve this situation is the development of what Feiman-Nemser and Buchmann have termed 'pedagogical thinking', or, put more simply, an awareness of 'how to build bridges between one's own understanding and that of one's students' (Feiman-Nemser and Buchmann, 1985: 6). Central to this process is the constructivist methodology described by Holt-Reynolds in terms of 'elicit[ing] student participation and then us[ing] students' existing ideas as a basis for helping them construct new, more reasoned, more accurate or more disciplined understandings' (Holt-Reynolds, 2000: 22). This constructivist approach – one that sees meaning as neither fixed and immutable, nor entirely subjective, but built instead through a collaborative and recursive process of exploration in which the teacher acts as a guiding and refining influence – is at the heart of all good literature teaching, and should underpin your approach to A Level.

Nevertheless, this process can only be fostered in the kind of classroom where students are used to engaging actively with their learning. You will need to establish yourself as the kind of teacher whose classes are a place for discussion and active engagement rather than spoon-feeding. This needs to happen from your very first encounter with your class, which will be just as important at A Level as it will be elsewhere in school.

What will you do in your first lesson? You might want to begin by getting your students to introduce themselves (or each other) and talk about their favourite book, an activity that might give you some intriguing insights into what they read beyond their A Level studies! Alternatively, you might want to provoke debate by giving them something controversial to discuss. One possibility is to get students to explore a number of deliberately provocative statements about reading, and ask them – in groups – to sort them into a continuum, from 'Agree strongly' to 'Disagree strongly'. Some possible statements are listed in the box below so you can try this yourself.

Activity 10.1

Attitudes towards reading

Sort the following statements into a continuum, from 'Agree strongly' to 'Disagree strongly'. Once you have done this, think carefully about the reasons for your choices and reflect on what this tells you about how you wish to approach teaching English Literature post-16.

- Everyone should have the chance to study Shakespeare at school.
- Analysing books in too much detail spoils them.
- Harry Potter is a better choice for today's young people than Jane Austen and Charles Dickens.
- It makes no sense to say that one book is 'better' than another.
- Poetry is much harder to understand than prose.
- Literature is about universal values and experiences that everyone can relate to.
- Reading makes you a better person.

Your plenary session should then get students to explore their views in more detail, challenging each others' ideas and responding to follow-up questions. An introductory activity like this will enable you to get to know your students and the way they think about books, and also to start to establish the foundations for analysing literature at A Level.

APPROACHES TO TEXTS

Let us turn now to the opening of *The Bell Jar*, where Sylvia Plath introduces us to her adolescent narrator – an overachieving scholarship girl who has won a competition to spend a summer in New York working as a fashion journalist. Read the first section of the text, from the beginning of the novel to '. . . the surrounding hullaballoo'. This section establishes the narrator's sense of dislocation from her environment, playing on our image of New York as a place of opportunity and excitement. How might you introduce students to this extract?

One possible starter activity is to get the students to explore their impressions of New York. A very simple way of doing this is to project the words 'New York' onto a white-board and ask students to record their images and impressions of this city on the board using marker pens, building up a shared spider diagram. (Some musical stimulus might help: try playing 'New York, New York' by Frank Sinatra, 'Empire State of Mind' by Alicia Keys or Duke Ellington's 'Harlem' while they are doing this!) This kind of activity is an excellent way of building students' engagement with a text: it provides an instant 'hook', gets them out of their seats, and encourages the sharing of ideas, using students' existing knowledge as a starting point.

The next step, of course, is to get your students to work with the extract itself. Will you get them to read it in silence, ask a student to read it out loud, or read it aloud yourself? You will probably use all of these methods at some point during the A Level course, but in these early stages, do not underestimate the power of your own voice to draw students into the text in this important first encounter. Think also about whether you will give your students any information about the text before you start, or focus their initial reading through giving them some questions to explore. The reading process will involve a number of exploratory steps before students can begin to analyse the text, as they orientate themselves in its 'world' and cope with vocabulary that might be unfamiliar to them. Sensitive questions – both closed and open – will help to guide them through this phase of their reading.

Activity 10.2

Questions

What kinds of knowledge will these questions generate? How will they help the students in their analysis of the text? Are there any questions that you wouldn't ask – or, alternatively, that you might add?

- What is happening in this extract? [How much information would you give students beforehand about the novel's historical and biographical context?]
- Who were the Rosenbergs?
- What is a cadaver?
- What is a bell jar? Why is this image significant?
- How has the narrator been spending her time in New York?
- How does she feel about the city?
- How does she think other people will view her?

Think next about how you will get them to annotate the extract so that they can explore its language in more detail. Students might have been introduced to the process of annotating texts at GCSE, but you will probably need to revisit this. A useful starting point is to ask them what kinds of features they look for when they annotate: are they picking out features of plot, character and theme, spotting techniques such as figurative language, recording their reactions to what they have read – or a mixture of all of these?

To build confidence in these early stages, it is often a good idea to build up a shared annotation of a text. This enables you to scaffold the annotation process, direct students' attention to particular features and use questions to prompt further thinking. Figure 10.1 offers some ideas for managing this process.

1. Project your text onto the whiteboard. Give each student a number of sticky notes. They have to write down anything they notice about the text and then stick their notes to the board. When they have finished, use their notes to explore the kinds of points they have made, noting recurring themes (and perhaps grouping these notes together) and asking further questions to get them to expand on their ideas. Using sticky notes allows students to remain relatively anonymous, which is particularly important in the early stages of the course when confidence might be shaky: it also gives them the freedom to say whatever they like.

2. Alternatively, give students whiteboard markers and ask them to record their observations on the whiteboard itself, underlining or highlighting significant words and phrases. This allows students to read and build on each others' points, and also encourages a focus on stylistic features. What can they say, for example, about Plath's use of two single-sentence paragraphs, or her recurring images of reflective surfaces?

3. You could also give students paper copies to annotate in pairs (photocopying extracts onto A3 paper, so that students have wide margins to write in, gives them scope to explore the text in detail). Once they have done this, you could get each pair to report back on a feature that they found particularly intriguing.

Figure 10.1 Teaching annotation skills

Note that what all of these activities do is to establish a pattern in which individual reflection and group work are followed by whole-class feedback and discussion – a process at the core of good English teaching. They could also be used in the early stages of teaching any literary text. Showalter (2003: 36–7) refers to the technique of 'teaching from the microcosm', in which the study of a long text begins with a focused exploration of a short extract that 'reveals how the author develops character, establishes tension [and] creates dramatic movement', thus allowing the student to 'read the rest of the [text] more insightfully' (Palmer, cited in Showalter: 37).

Activity 10.3

Use of key extracts

Think of the texts you know well: which extracts might you select to exemplify a moment of crisis, a key point of character development, or the author's characteristic use of language? (And think also of how you could use this technique with poetry or drama: its use is not confined to prose.)

CONTEXTS AND CRITICS

Until the end of the twentieth century, A Level English Literature was experienced by many students as revolving around a traditional triumvirate of character, theme and language, a situation likened by the critic Robert Eaglestone to 'studying biology in the way your grandparents did' (Eaglestone, 1999). The reforms of A Level English Literature that have taken place since the introduction of Curriculum 2000 have attempted to draw on the advances in critical and cultural theory that have taken place in university departments of English, closing the gap between A Level and HE. Students now have to deal with concepts such as genre, narrative and representation, thinking about the 'constructedness' of texts rather than seeing them as a simple reflection of 'real life': they also have to 'demonstrate understanding of the significance and influence of the contexts in which literary texts are written and received', and explore the ways in which texts have been interpreted by other readers (QCA, 2006: 6). You will need to think about how to address these requirements in your teaching, so that students experience them as genuinely empowering, rather than constrictive and bewildering.

Let us look at the requirement to show an understanding of the contexts in which literary texts are written and received. Of course, it would be possible to tackle this by giving students reams of 'background reading' in the form of biographical and historical material, but this runs the risk of baffling your students: such material might well end up misunderstood and unassimilated, if indeed it is read at all. It is often far more effective to drip-feed small amounts of information and ask students to reflect on how this contributes to their understanding of specific aspects of a text.

Activity 10.4

Working with context

Look at the following statements. How could you get your students to use this material to illuminate their reading of the extract from *The Bell Jar*?

- *The Bell Jar* was originally published under the pseudonym 'Victoria Lucas', and was not published in the US until 1971. The novel draws very closely on events in Plath's own life.
- Plath was a student at Smith College, a prestigious all-girls' school in Massachusetts, where she was an extremely high achiever. In her essay 'America! America!' Plath wrote 'I was just too dangerously brainy. My high, pure string of straight As might, without proper, extra-curricular tempering, snap me into the void. More and more, the colleges wanted All-Round Students' (Plath, 1977: 36).
- In the summer of 1953 Plath spent three months in New York as a guest editor for the magazine *Mademoiselle*. Her supervising editor described her as 'stiff and formal' and 'incapable of spontaneity' (Gould, 2011).
- Plath's diary entry of 14 July 1953 reads: 'All right, you have gone the limit – you tried today, after 2 hours only of sleep for the last two nights, to shut yourself off from responsibility altogether: you looked around and saw everybody either married or busy and happy and thinking and being creative, and you felt scared, sick, lethargic, worst of all, not wanting to cope. . . . You must not . . . shut walls up between you & the world & all the gay bright girls' (Kukil, 2000: 186–7).
- The Cold War era in the USA has been described as a time when roles for middle-class women were conservative and prescriptive, enforcing conformity on women rather than allowing them to explore the kinds of opportunities that were available to men. The writer Emily Gould has stated that in 1950s America 'intelligence and ambition, past a certain threshold, were real liabilities for women' (Gould, 2011). Rosi Smith has commented that 'Plath and her protagonist came of age in an era where women were explicitly told that happiness could only be achieved through the enactment of a biological imperative, in a society in which all deviance was treated with suspicion' (Smith, 2008).

Activity 10.4 *continued*

- Julius and Ethel Rosenberg were executed by electric chair in June 1953 for passing US nuclear secrets to the USSR. Sylvia Plath received electric shock therapy for depression when she was in her early 20s. In *The Bell Jar*, Esther also receives this treatment. Mental health campaigners have used *The Bell Jar* as an example of the barbaric treatment given in the past to people in psychiatric hospitals.

These statements could be used in a number of ways. You could put students in pairs and give each pair one piece of contextual information to consider before reporting back to the rest of the group; or give the students all the statements and ask them to choose the one they consider most important (and justify their choice). Later, you could ask students to find and add their own pieces of information: if you give them a tight word limit, or ask them to write their information on an index card, this will avoid the printing-off of reams of Wikipedia that contextual research can easily become if you are not careful. You will, of course, be able to adapt this activity for use with other texts that require an awareness of historical and biographical context. *Jane Eyre* is one obvious example. What would you want students to know about Charlotte Brontë's own life, the situation of women in nineteenth-century England, or about early critical reactions to *Jane Eyre*? At what stage might you introduce this contextual information? And how would you get your students to make use of it?

Creative assessment

You might want to get your students to write up their analysis of this extract, since this will allow you to make a first assessment of their ability to express their ideas in writing and alert you to any difficulties they might have. Nevertheless, this unit of work also contains a number of opportunities for more imaginative forms of assessment. You could get your students to:

- work in groups to turn their annotated version of the text into a poster, including images, biographical and contextual information, and thoughts on the text;
- summarise their ideas on one particular aspect of the text in the form of a spoken presentation, or a seminar in which they pose questions for other students to discuss;
- produce a 'Reader's Guide' to the text that would act as an introductory guide for others;
- contribute to a discussion about the text on your VLE, responding to prompts that you have posted and engaging with each others' ideas.

You should also ask students to consider the contexts within which they read the text. Would the extract from *The Bell Jar* work in the same way if the reader was not aware of the stereotypical images of New York that they shared at the beginning of this unit? And what about the enduring popularity of *The Bell Jar*, which Emily Gould describes as 'a touchstone for a certain kind of introspective, moody teenager'? There's an interesting discussion to be had here about why people are drawn to novels about trauma, and to the 'misery memoirs' that have become a publishing phenomenon in recent years. This kind of discussion will add to the richness of students' A Level experience, enabling them to make connections between the work they do in class and the wider culture in which books are circulated, mediated and consumed.

Similar approaches can be used when exploring the interpretations of other readers. Be attentive to the requirements of your particular specification: some ask students to refer to named critics, following academic conventions of referencing, while others are happy with a more general discussion of possible interpretations. One activity that works particularly well is to present students with a range of quotations from different sources (an exercise that is especially effective with a text that polarises critical opinion, such as *The Merchant of Venice*, or the poetry of Philip Larkin). They could rank these quotations in order of how strongly they agree with them, find evidence to support them, choose one that they disagree with and formulate a counter-argument. As with the study of contextual information, prioritise the quality of students' engagement over the quantity of reading they do. The English and Media Centre publication *Text, Reader, Critic* offers some excellent suggestions for ways of introducing students to the idea that texts can be interpreted in different ways, and to some different schools of criticism.

Planning activities like this is where your knowledge of the text interacts with your growing awareness of pedagogy – identifying what your students need to know, defining appropriate learning objectives and planning activities that will be both stimulating and challenging to scaffold their understanding of the text. Think, for instance, of how you could use online word-cloud generators such as Wordle or Tagxedo to encourage students to focus on language and its connotations (exploring a word-cloud is a fantastic starter activity, and a very effective way of easing students into complex texts that might otherwise seem overwhelming). Equally, you might embark on your study of a novel or play by presenting students with a series of quotations relating to a major character, and asking them what they can deduce about this character from an initial close reading of these extracts. I've used this method with a range of texts, from *Hamlet* to *The Great Gatsby*, *Enduring Love* and *Birdsong*, and it encourages students to speculate, make connections and engage with the text in a very focused manner. An example can be seen at Figure 10.2.

Figure 10.2 Enduring Love word-cloud

CONCLUSIONS

Embarking on your first full-length set text will be daunting, especially if you are teaching a long novel. Teaching a literary text at A Level is like climbing a mountain: a matter of working towards a long-term goal by way of a series of short-term objectives that provide handholds, footholds and staging points along the way. Simon Gibbons describes this process as:

> about relating individual lessons into the 'bigger picture' of the study of a text or a group of related texts and – simultaneously – about linking day to day work with the overarching knowledge and skills in terms of developing as a critical reader and as a student able to confidently negotiate the assessment hurdles.
>
> (Gibbons, 2010: 8)

You will need to think carefully about how you will shape and direct this process, considering how your students are going to 'get the reading done', how you will scaffold their learning outside the classroom, and how you will develop their independence as readers.

Crucially, however, you should also remember to convey in your A Level teaching your own enthusiasm for your subject, your love of reading and your sense of English Literature as a subject that should not be limited to – or by – what goes on in the classroom. The educationalist John Hattie (2008: 238) has written of the importance of being openly 'switched on' by one's subject – of being a 'passionate, accomplished teacher' who is alive to the moment and able to respond to the directions that students' thinking might take. Such teachers shape not only their students' learning, but also their relationship with literature itself: to occupy this role is to be in an extremely privileged position.

RECOMMENDED READING

Cowell, C. and Layton, N. (2006) *That Rabbit Belongs to Emily Brown*. London: Orchard.

Eaglestone, R. (1999) 'A critical time for English'. *Guardian*. Available at http://www.guardian.co.uk/education/1999/nov/30/schools.theguardian1

Feiman-Nemser, S. and Buchmann, M. (1985) The first year of teacher preparation: transition to pedagogical thinking?, *Research Series*, 156. East Lansing: Michigan State University, Institute for Research on Teaching.

Gibbons, S. (2010) 'Literature Study Post-16 Part 2. ITE English: Readings for Discussion'. Available at http://www.ite.org.uk/ite_readings/literature_p16_II_20100303.pdf

Gould, E. (2011) 'The Bell Jar at 40'. Available at http://www.poetryfoundation.org/article/242402

Hattie, J. (2008) *Visible Learning*. London: Routledge.

Holt-Reynolds, D. (2000) 'What does the teacher do? Constructivist pedagogies and prospective teachers' beliefs about the role of a teacher', *Teaching and Teacher Education*, 16: 21–32.

Jacobs, R. (2010) 'English Literature Post-16 Part 1. ITE English: Readings for Discussion'. Available at http://www.ite.org.uk/ite_readings/literature_p16_I_20100303.pdf

Kukil, K. V. (2000) *The Journals of Sylvia Plath, 1950–1962*. London: Faber & Faber.

McCormick, K. (1994) *The Culture of Reading and the Teaching of English*. Manchester: Manchester University Press.

Plath, S. (1963) *The Bell Jar*. London: Heinemann.

Plath, S. (1977) *Johnny Panic and the Bible of Dreams*. London: Faber & Faber.

QCA (2006) 'GCE AS and A-level subject criteria for English literature'. Available at http://www.ofqual.gov.uk/files/qca-06-2850_english_literature.pdf

Showalter, E. (2003) *Teaching Literature*. Oxford: Blackwell.

Smith, R. (2008) 'Seeing Through the Bell Jar: Distorted Female Identity in Cold War America'. Available at http://www.aspeers.com/2008/smith?fulltext

Chapter 11 Teaching English using ICT

JAMES SHEA

In this chapter you will:

- consider your personal experiences and views of teaching English using ICT;
- reflect on ICT texts and ICT subject knowledge;
- consider what you hope to achieve through the teaching of English using ICT;
- think about the range of ICT texts in English;
- explore a number of pedagogic approaches to the teaching of English using ICT.

INTRODUCTION

The teaching of English using ICT can be challenging because it requires secondary subject knowledge. How can you ask pupils to write a Facebook profile for *Romeo and Juliet* if you have never used Facebook? What grammatical rules are followed for blogging? If someone joins video and writing together, is it still creative writing? What technology should you employ in the classroom as opposed to taking the class to an ICT room? All of these questions have rapidly evolved in a short space of time and it is important that you have answers to these questions. Just as it is the English teacher who contextualises the use of racist language in *Of Mice and Men* or *To Kill a Mockingbird*, so it is the English teacher who contextualises the language contained in new forms of expressions such as tweets or Facebook posts.

In reality, these questions or variants on them have challenged English teachers for a long time – so, although it may require additional knowledge of ICT and digital literacy, the evolution of language through technology has always fascinated the profession and it can be used to inspire and teach pupils to see English as the modern and vibrant subject it is.

The main starting point for you must be to reflect on what knowledge and skills you start with and whether you could enhance your potential teaching through the development of your ICT skills.

Activity 11.1

Thinking about ICT

Work through the reflective questions below. Be prepared to isolate clear targets for yourself with regards skills or knowledge.

Activity 11.1 *continued*

1   What is your general attitude to technology? Have you always been interested in the latest gadget? Do you own an iPad, a Kindle or a Smartphone? When you operate the projector or the interactive whiteboard in the classroom are you confident and assured or hesitant and avoid them?

2   How do you feel about electronic writing versus handwritten pieces? Do you see them as different – like books and films – or do you see one as superior to another?

3   What examples have you seen of teachers using ICT in the classroom? Is it limited to the typing up of work or have you seen group projects involving Virtual Learning Environments and online publishing?

4   What do you want to achieve by using ICT in your classroom? Better writing? Improved reading? To inspire pupils who are not responding to traditional means?

5   Is your vision of teaching English with ICT one of pupils typing up their work or is it one of collaboration and online publication?

VIEWS OF ICT

ICT has moved paradigmatically in the last five years with the advent of Web 2.0. This is a technical term relating to how interactive the form of ICT is. A webpage that contains only text, images or video for the audience passively to read is Web 1.0 By adding a 'comment' section, we make it interactive. By allowing contributors to see each other's comments and interact with each other and the text we make it Web 2.0. You can take this premise and transport it to your own teaching. Place a poem or an extract from a key text on a school's virtual learning environment (VLE) and allow comments to be made. However, completing this technical action is insufficient to generate learning. You now have to teach pupils to make high quality comments – to cite, to use appropriate terminology, to balance their argument, to take on board and develop others' ideas – in short, to teach good quality writing. Thus, the building blocks of good writing stay the same, but the opportunities to use them have evolved as technology has grown over the years.

Developing this theme allows you to see how ICT can be viewed. It can be seen as a passive 're-presenter' of information – to make information neat and more effectively presented than previously. However, this would be a rather limited use of the technology. In order to capture its bigger possibilities, ICT really needs to be seen as an engine that drives collaborative and interactive communication and work. As Franklin and van Harmelin (2007: 4) observe, 'With Web 2.0 data sharing the web also becomes a platform for social software that enables groups of users to socialise collaborate and work with each other.' Thus, if you see your pupils as a learning community who use technology to collaborate and engage with each other's work – using Assessment for Learning (AfL) principles – then you can begin to use ICT to teach English more effectively whilst at the same time harness the transferable skills your pupils have developed through using ICT outside of the classroom.

THE CHANGING WORLD OF TECHNOLOGY

Teaching English with ICT has moved beyond using Microsoft Word, PowerPoint or Publisher to re-present content which was previously presented using other media (like conventional whiteboards or on paper). Teaching English with ICT means embracing the nature of collaboration, of frequent peer assessment, modern publishing opportunities and recognising that all of these modern practices still require high quality English skills –

writing, reading, critiquing, communication, remodelling and so forth – and that these skills need to be taught in context.

Creative assessment: Using a scenario

Think about how you would introduce the following scenario to a class in a way which ensured that the key English skills required by the scenario are addressed. Consider how it could be explored in your classroom. How would you encourage pupils to consider the questions faced by the poet?

A poet wishes to develop an audience without going to a publisher. He or she has decided to run a simple website with a daily blog that can be accessed through an app, email or the website, a weekly newsletter sent out by email, a Facebook home page, two or three poems a week with comments from readers allowed and a Twitter account. Their first volume of poetry is available through Kindle's self-publishing site.

- As a poet self-publishing through Kindle, what are the forms and conventions of a published book that need to be adhered to – layout, structure, etc?
- What are the expectations of the audience when it comes to a daily blog?
- What information and interactive elements would readers expect from a weekly newsletter?
- What kind of censorship and editorial control needs to be introduced to ensure readers' poems are suitable?
- What would the content of regular tweets look like?

Sitting alongside the use of surface technology, you would need your pupils to write for a particular audience using appropriate language and conventions, to be able to write and critique poetry, to write reflectively on themes similar to the poems, to be able to draw on the Twitter-like qualities of brevity of the Haiku canon (non-negotiable short length pieces) and 'tweet' effectively within a limited number of characters. On top of this is an understanding of modern marketing methodology – the ability to fuse social networking promotion with the commercialisation of texts. Modern authors involve their audience with their texts through interactive means – J. K. Rowling has launched http://www.pottermore.com to achieve exactly that aim.

By interspersing the teaching of key writing skills with group work and embedding the technology within homework and use of the school's ICT resources, you could ensure that pupils develop a strong set of skills such as analysis, knowledge of exam specific poems, collaborative work and the notion of published writing with its emphasis on accuracy and precision. This last notion is not one to be dismissed lightly. One of the main dangers that young pupils face is the fact that much of what they write (on social networking sites, etc.) is in the public domain. This means that there is much more pressure on pupils to know how to write effectively and to create a strong impression through their 'online public identity' – one aspect you must consider is the idea that your pupils are already frequently reading and writing online and without guidance and support they could negatively affect their futures. At the very least, the notion of *safe online communication* should be embedded into your teaching. Childnet, (http://www.childnet-int.org/safety/teachers.aspx) is an organisation that can help provide resources for the English teacher. As Childnet says:

> many parents assume that issues of Internet safety are being taught in the school where Internet access is safe. Teachers therefore, should be encouraged to play a more proactive role in educating parents about keeping their children safe online to help ensure that good safe school use of the Internet is mirrored by good safe out of school use.
>
> (Childnet, 2011)

What you will rapidly perceive, is that as a beginning teacher you have to maintain an up-to-date knowledge of the impact that technology is having on the world of language and literature. Being up to date means that you can then teach the core skills and abilities your pupils will need in order to communicate in a variety of ways beyond the school classroom. The idea of communication is key here – Information Technology has become Information and *Communication* Technology. The largest change in recent years has been the exponential increase in the amount of online communication, which has led to the formation of 'instant' and long-term communities. In 2009, Neilson found that email was no longer the most popular communication medium – instead, social networking sites were. Today's pupil needs to be taught how to construct letters and emails, but also other ways of communicating – such as through social networking. This includes addressing the forms and conventions of such genres in all the same ways as traditional letter writing. It is also important to address the dangers of such forms of communication – for example, libel, impressions on future employers, identity theft and even how a Facebook post can lead to a four-year prison sentence for 'incitement to riot'!

ICT AND LITERACY

As English teachers, you have a statutory duty to ensure that your pupils experience their entitlement in education – drawn from the NC and the National Frameworks (http://curriculum.qcda.gov.uk). This can be overwhelming for young pupils as they struggle to cope with the proliferating demands of language, literature and media that exist in society. Teaching with ICT helps pupils to relate to notions of genre (as more and more genres are spawned), and to approach their varied forms and conventions through high quality S&L, reading, writing and analysis – the core skills at the heart of good English teaching. What, though, is the relationship between ICT and literacy – is there evidence that it makes pupils lazy and less literate?

The Evidence for Policy and Practice Information and Co-ordinating Centre (EPPI-Centre – http://eppi.ioe.ac.uk/cms) at the Institute for Education, University of London reviewed 56 papers in a study into teaching English with ICT. Results were non-conclusive: there was simply not enough high quality research available to answer their questions. However, they did state that:

> In practice terms, ICT is best seen as another tool in the repertoire available to learners and teachers for expression and communication. Custom-made word-processing and other software programs should be considered by teachers, as some of these prove to be more attuned to the writing process than others. Teachers also need to be aware that there are times when the use of ICT is appropriate for a particular writing task (or part of that task), and other times when different media are more appropriate. Continued and prolonged exposure to ICT can be demotivating.
>
> (Andrews, R. *et al.*, 2005: 13)

Activity 11.2

ICT and literacy

Think about the EPPI report, and then respond to the following questions. Where do you stand on the debate of using ICT in the classroom and why you have formed these opinions?

Activity 11.2 *continued*

- Does typing into a word processor or text editor with synchronous computer-aided spelling and grammar checking prevent a pupil's literacy from being developed?
- Are some types of reading texts superior to others?
- Should a pupil only type their written response if there is a specific reason to do so?
- Is too much technology in the classroom a bad thing? What is too much?

The last question opens up a new field for consideration. What exactly is technology in the classroom? Traditionally, it has been the preserve of desktops and laptops for pupils and teachers with either projection or inputting taking place. Increasingly, interactive whiteboards have taken a place in the classroom, but in some ways these can be seen as a large, publicly displayed laptop or desktop. However, you will notice that mobile technology has started to push its way into the classroom. Smartphones and tablet computers have clear advantages over cumbersome laptops and desktops – and not just in mobility terms.

USE OF MOBILE TECHNOLOGIES

Today's mobile devices come with the ability to tap into the burgeoning 'app' market. Need a rhyming poetry word? There is a fistful of apps offering this service for free. Need a dictionary or thesaurus? With working examples? Again – these apps exist for both the Android market and the iPhone/iPad market. The advantage of these apps is that they tap straight into web-based material and thus are unlimited in what they can offer. They can offer modelling, video explanations, alternative approaches and a variety of ways of enhancing pupils' work. Why would a poet or creative writer not use technology in their work? For pupils with additional needs, app-based mobile technology can be a fantastic source of help and information. Pupils can take a photo of a text and have an instant translator turn the text into a different language. They can download apps to help them learn specific areas of English such as grammar or expression. What pupils struggle with is learning how to embed English related technology into their processes. How do they use it? When should they use it? How do they know if what they are using is of a high quality or not? Once again, we see that core English skills need to be taught alongside the use of technology so that when the pupil is outside the classroom they learn to synthesise and differentiate correctly.

To teach English successfully using ICT requires you to see it as more than a tool for 're-presenting' in a different format information which pupils have traditionally written by hand. Whilst technology can help pupils present their ideas using a wide range of multimodal outputs as well as traditional word processing, the real advantages lie in shaping your pupils' skills and knowledge through employing the ICT which they frequently use in their time outside of lessons.

SPECIFIC TECHNOLOGY

It is important that you assess what kind of ICT is available to you as an English teacher. Schools have traditionally created ICT rooms which are sometimes part of the ICT department, or sometimes there is an ICT suite dedicated to a subject area. The advantages of having an English-specific ICT room for the department are that staff can personalise the room and machines to meet pupils' needs in English, become more familiar with the technological maintenance of the equipment, and utilise some of the excellent software available. For example, LanSchool software (http://www.lanschool.com) enables the teacher to turn the internet or browser on and off for all the computers in the room. It lets the teacher freeze every screen and send messages to all pupils. The teacher can take control of a single machine from the teacher's desk or even display a single pupil's work on all machines or on the IWB. Such control enables an English teacher to embed good pedagogy such as peer assessment into teaching. However, to use such a room requires a teacher to book the room in advance. For this to be effective, you will need to consider this in your medium and long-term planning. When writing a Scheme of Work for your classes, consider if time in an ICT room would be beneficial and book it accordingly in advance.

In addition to ICT rooms many schools have banks of equipment that are either held centrally or departmentally – these may include laptops and a range of mobile learning devices. They may be simple MP3 recorders or more advanced mini-video cameras such as the Flipcam. We tend to group such devices into the category of 'capture devices'.

Many times, in an English lesson, you will create fantastic work with your class – wonderful in-depth discussions, insightful tableaux or drama pieces and in-depth mind maps or brain storms. At the end of the lesson or activity, this work can easily disappear and lose its power to impact on further teaching and learning. Using ICT capture devices as part of your English teaching means that you can keep the work so it can continue to have an impact – perhaps as an *aide memoire* to stimulate later discussion, as the basis for interim assessments, or for inclusion in future pieces of work. Drama can be videoed, tableaux and brain storms can be photographed, discussions can be recorded – and all of this content placed into the school's VLE to be accessed by pupils at a later date. Pupils are often confident and experienced at capturing experiences using multimedia and so to do so for educational purposes harnesses these transferable skills and helps to advance their English skills.

It is also important to think about how you will use the school's VLE. Good practice is to embed the VLE into your teaching at the planning stage. If you know you are going to discuss, for example, the theme of racism in Shakespeare's *The Merchant of Venice*, then place a thread in a discussion forum ready for pupils to contribute their ideas and refer to the online thread in the classroom as part of your teaching. You can also create projects or pages around key areas for pupils to populate as part of their group work. Thus, the pupils can work in your lessons on content that they will use to populate the online project area as part of their work either at home or in the ICT room. For example, you might be studying William Blake's *Songs of Innocence and of Experience* with an A Level group. You could divide the poems into pairs and allocate several pairs of poems to each group asking them to populate the online project area with background research, close textual analysis, their own opinions and the opinions of others. Once this has been done, not only is there a terrific resource for current and future pupils, but the pupils have learned key English skills using collaborative techniques.

Activity 11.3

Employing ICT

How would you embed ICT into your Scheme of Work to enable the following outcomes to be met?

1   *KS3* – Your pupils are reading *Holes* by Louis Sachar and are exploring the key themes of relationships, crime and punishment. You want them to

Activity 11.3 *continued*

apply modern news items to the novel and explore how relevant the novel is to their lives today. Writing is a target for this class as their literacy lets them down.

2 *KS4* – Your pupils are studying *creative writing* – learning to create good copy at speed for their controlled assessment task. You want them to be able to write fiction or non-fiction and to be able to use each other to drive up the standards of their written work. This class needs to be able to match audience to style more effectively.

3 *Post-16* – Your pupils are studying and comparing Aphra Behn's *The Rover*, a restoration play from the 1660s, with *Wuthering Heights* by Emily Brontë. More emphasis is placed on *Wuthering Heights* with *The Rover* being a companion text. Your pupils are focused on comparing the two texts for their insights into the representation of women in literature. This class must develop their ability to work and research independently in preparation for the final module and HE in general.

INTERACTIVE WHITEBOARDS (IWB) AND PROJECTORS

Nearly all classrooms now have at least a projector if not an IWB. As you might guess, it is an excellent opportunity to pre-prepare materials for lessons that would otherwise take up your time in the classroom if you had to write them on the board – time that can be spent teaching instead. At a simple level this can be things like learning objectives, lesson outcomes or modelled sentence starters. You can also reinforce oral instructions with written instructions on screen – and there are sound pedagogical reasons for doing this. Simply having instructions repeated on the screen enables latecomers, pupils with attention deficit needs, hearing-impaired pupils, English as Additional Language (EAL) learners and those who struggle to pay attention such as non-aural learners to engage more effectively with classroom activities leading to smoother transitions and teaching.

As you begin to use the IWB and projector more effectively, so you can put up extracts for you and the class to annotate. Pupils sometimes struggle accurately to visualise what it is they have to do, so using the IWB to demonstrate can be of great assistance. Treating the IWB or projector as an oversized teacher's desk enables your pupils to see exactly what it is you wish them to do. As you highlight, annotate and model the use of appropriate terminology, so you will find your pupils mirror this on their own extracts. In some ways, it sets the bar for the standard of work you wish to see – it is modelling the process, not just the finished product. By harnessing the interactive possibilities of the IWB or projector, it is possible to build the use of other technology into your teaching of English. You can show parts of the school's VLE, the class wiki, work previously produced by the class and captured. Even live video can be captured for immediate playback so that groups producing drama or tableaux can perform self-assessment.

CONCLUSIONS

Teaching English using ICT has evolved just as rapidly as technology has. The presence of ICT in classrooms and the extent to which departments use it varies from school to school, but you cannot escape the fact that you are preparing pupils for the modern world. A strong emphasis on teaching core English skills contextualised within modern technology is the right way forward. As a beginning teacher, being able to harness each new development in ICT to assist your own teaching should be a regular part of your subject knowledge and professional development keeping English as a subject fresh, modern and vibrant.

RECOMMENDED READING

Adams, A. and Brindley, S. (eds) (2011) *Teaching Secondary English with ICT*. Maidenhead: Open University Press.

Andrews, R., Dan, H., Freeman, A., McGuinn, N., Robinson, A. and Zhu, D. (2005) The effectiveness of different ICTs in the teaching and learning of English (written composition), 5–16, in *Research Evidence in Education Library*. London: EPPI-Centre, Social Science Research Unit, Institute of Education, University of London.

Arnesen, T. (2011) *The Role of ICT in the Teaching of English as a Foreign Language EFL*. Saarbrücken: LAP Lambert Academic Publishing AG & Co KG.

Childnet (2011) 'Teacher's. Available at http://www.childnet-int.org/safety/teachers.aspx (accessed 04/09/2011).

Franklin, T., and Van Harmelin, M. (2007) *Web 2.0 for learning and teaching in higher education*. London: The Observatory of Borderless Higher Education. Available at http://ie-repository.jisc.ac.uk/148/1/web2-content-learning-and-teaching.pdf

Nielson, (2009) *Global Places and Networked Faces: A Nielsen report on Social Networking's New Global Footprint*. Available at http://blog.nielsen.com/nielsenwire/wp-content/uploads/2009/03/nielsen_globalfaces_mar09.pdf (accessed 09/03/2009).

Pachler, N. and Daly, C. (2011) *Key Issues in eLearning: research and practice*. New York: Continuum.

Warren, C., Millum, T. and Rank, T. (2011) *Teaching English using ICT*. New York: Continuum.

Index